TRACKS AND TASTES A CULINARY JOURNEY THROUGH INDIAN RAILWAY CATERING

TRACKS AND TASTES A CULINARY JOURNEY THROUGH INDIAN RAILWAY CATERING

MACK RAFEAL

UNIEK ENTERPRISES

CONTENTS

INDEX

Introduction

Introduction

The musical bang of wheels on tracks and the pleasant whistle of a far off train inspire a feeling of sentimentality for the majority, conjuring recollections of train ventures across the tremendous and different scene of India. Past the grand vistas and the kinship of individual voyagers, one part of these excursions makes a permanent imprint on the faculties — the culinary odyssey through Indian Railroad cooking.

As the train leaves from clamoring stations and winds its direction through the open country, the fragrance of flavors and the sizzle of cooking drift through the air. The culinary excursion starts when the storeroom vehicle springs to life, its kitchen a clamoring very busy place where gourmet specialists coordinate an ensemble of flavors that epitomizes the quintessence of India's different culinary legacy.

One can't set out on a culinary endeavor on Indian Rail routes without experiencing the omnipresent 'chai wallahs' who navigate the length of the train, their provincial streetcars weighed down with steaming cups of chai. The unquestionable smell of masala chai, a mix of sweet-smelling flavors areas of strength for and tea, saturates the air as travelers enthusiastically anticipate their chance to enjoy this quintessential Indian refreshment.

Moving past the consoling hug of chai, the storage space vehicle divulges an embroidery of local dishes that reflects the social kaleidoscope of the country. From the hot extravagance of Vindaloo in Goa to the flavorful Dhokla of Gujarat, the menu offers a gastronomic excursion that reflects the geological variety of the Indian subcontinent.

North Indian rarities, portrayed by rich sauces and fragrant flavors, show up. The fragrant biryanis, delicious kebabs, and rich margarine chicken act as envoys of the vigorous and tasty cooking that has its foundations in the prolific fields of the Ganges.

As the train adventures toward the south, the menu goes through a change, acquainting the sense of taste with the tart kinds of tamarind, coconut, and curry leaves. The red hot Chettinad curries of Tamil Nadu and the tart rasam of Karnataka offer a glaring difference to the milder, cream-based curries of the north. Each chomp is a demonstration of the culinary variety that flourishes in the southern spans of the subcontinent.

The beach front stretches of India contribute their own oceanic abundance to the railroad menu. New fish, got from the Bedouin Ocean and Narrows of Bengal, tracks down its direction onto the plates of anxious travelers. From the famous fish curry of Kerala to the fiery prawn masala of West Bengal, the rail line catering embraces the beach front fortunes that have supported networks for a really long time.

Vegan delights, frequently eclipsed by their substantial partners, guarantee a noticeable put on the rail line menu. The humble yet generous lentil-based dishes like Dal Tadka and Rajma Chawal grandstand the adaptability of veggie lover cooking in India. Every locale confers its special curve to these veggie lover works of art, bringing about a mixture of flavors that take care of different preferences.

The railroad catering experience isn't restricted to local strengths alone; it stretches out to the mutual eating experience that unfurls inside the limits of the train. The musical clunking of steel plates and the murmur of discussion make a mood that rises above the actual limits of the feasting vehicle. Outsiders become eating buddies, sharing stories and suggestions over a spread that joins them in the normal delight of good food.

The culinary excursion through Indian Rail lines isn't just about the objective; it is tied in with appreciating the nuanced orchestra of tastes that reverberation the social extravagance of the land. In the midst of the culinary enjoyments, one can't overlook the calculated wonder that empowers this gastronomic odyssey. The storage space vehicle, a versatile kitchen on wheels, works with accuracy to take special care of the culinary necessities of many travelers rushing across the immense scope of the subcontinent.

The difficulties of keeping up with quality and consistency in a moving kitchen are met with creativity and commitment. Cooks explore restricted spaces and time limitations to guarantee that each dish is a demonstration of the culinary mastery that characterizes Indian food. The storage room vehicle is a demonstration of the flexibility and creativity of Indian Railroads, changing the moving train into a versatile café that rivals fixed foundations in its culinary contributions.

The culinary undertaking through Indian Rail routes isn't restricted to the bounds of the storage space vehicle. At different stations, nearby merchants offer a variety of road food that entices travelers to appreciate the kinds of the area. From the fiery 'chaat' of Delhi to the flavorful 'vada pav' of Mumbai, the stages change into outdoors showcases where travelers can leave on a gastronomic experience while the train makes a concise stop.

Past the provincial strengths and road food guilty pleasures, the railroad cooking menu likewise takes special care of the worldwide sense of taste. As India develops as a worldwide center, the culinary contributions on trains mirror a receptiveness to global flavors.

Pasta, noodles, and mainland breakfast choices track down a spot close by conventional Indian charge, furnishing travelers with a different exhibit of decisions that reflect the cosmopolitan idea of contemporary India.

The culinary excursion through Indian Rail routes isn't without its snapshots of luck. The opportunity experiences with nearby sellers, the extemporaneous discussions with individual travelers, and the common delight of a very much prepared dinner add to an encounter that rises above the simple demonstration of eating. It turns into a festival of variety, a demonstration of the solidarity that can be tracked down in the common joy of eating together.

1. **Overview of Indian Railway Catering**

   Indian Rail route Cooking is a culinary endeavor that rises above the bounds of customary feasting, offering travelers a gastronomic odyssey across the tremendous and different scene of India. The rail route catering experience isn't simply about the objective; it is an excursion of the faculties, an ensemble of tastes that mirrors the social extravagance of the subcontinent. As the train sets out on its excursion, the culinary endeavor starts, unfurling inside the bounds of the storage room vehicle, a versatile kitchen on wheels that changes the moving train into a culinary shelter.

   The core of the railroad providing food activity lies in the storage space vehicle, a calculated wonder that explores the difficulties of keeping up with quality and consistency in a versatile kitchen. Cooks work with accuracy and commitment to organize a culinary ensemble that catches the substance of India's different culinary legacy. In this restricted space, the gourmet specialists explore restricted living arrangements and time imperatives, guaranteeing that each dish is a demonstration of the culinary skill that characterizes Indian food.

   The menu, a cautiously organized determination of local claims to fame, road food extravagances, and worldwide flavors, reflects the geological and social variety of the subcontinent. From the vigorous and tasty flavors of North Indian food to the tart and zesty contributions of the south, the railroad cooking menu is a mixture of tastes that takes special care of the different palates of travelers crossing the far reaching scene.

   The universal 'chai wallahs' assume a significant part in the culinary excursion, crossing the length of the train with natural streetcars loaded down with steaming cups of masala chai. The unmistakable fragrance of this quintessential Indian refreshment, a mix of sweet-smelling flavors areas of strength for and tea, consumes the space as travelers enthusiastically anticipate their chance to enjoy this soothing remedy. Past chai, the storage space vehicle discloses an embroidery of flavors, acquainting travelers with provincial dishes that grandstand the culinary kaleidoscope of the country.

   North Indian treats, known for their rich sauces and fragrant flavors, show up on the menu. Delicious kebabs, fragrant biryanis, and smooth margarine chicken act as representatives of the strong food that starts from the prolific fields of the Ganges. As the train adventures toward the south, the menu goes through a change, embracing the tart kinds of tamarind, coconut, and curry leaves. The blazing Chettinad curries of Tamil Nadu and the tart rasam of Karnataka offer a glaring difference to the milder, cream-based curries of the north.

Waterfront extends contribute their sea abundance to the rail route menu, highlighting new fish got from the Bedouin Ocean and Cove of Bengal. From the notable fish curry of Kerala to the hot prawn masala of West Bengal, the railroad catering embraces the waterfront prizes that have supported networks for quite a long time. Vegan delights guarantee an unmistakable put on the menu, displaying the flexibility of lentils and vegetables in dishes like Dal Tadka and Rajma Chawal. Every locale gives its exceptional bend to these vegan works of art, bringing about a mixture of flavors that take special care of different preferences.

The culinary excursion reaches out past the bounds of the storage room vehicle to the common feasting experience that unfurls inside the train. The cadenced ringing of steel plates and the murmur of discussion make a mood that rises above the actual limits of the eating vehicle. Outsiders become feasting colleagues, sharing stories and suggestions over a spread that joins them in the normal delight of good food. It is a festival of variety, a demonstration of the solidarity tracked down in the common joy of eating together.

The difficulties of working a versatile kitchen on wheels are met with resourcefulness and devotion. The storage room vehicle, with its painstakingly coordinated kitchen and talented gourmet experts, guarantees that travelers experience a consistent and luscious culinary excursion. The strategic wonder of furnishing many travelers with a different and top notch menu while rushing across the huge field of the subcontinent is a demonstration of the versatility and genius of Indian Rail routes.

The rail route catering experience isn't restricted to the storeroom vehicle alone. At different stations, nearby sellers offer a variety of road food that allures travelers to appreciate the kinds of the locale. The stages change into outside business sectors where travelers can set out on a gastronomic experience while the train makes a short stop. From the zesty 'chaat' of Delhi to the flavorful 'vada pav' of Mumbai, these improvised experiences with neighborhood sellers add an additional layer of genuineness to the culinary excursion.

As India develops as a worldwide center point, the culinary contributions on trains mirror a receptiveness to global flavors. Pasta, noodles, and mainland breakfast choices track down a spot close by customary Indian toll, giving travelers a different exhibit of decisions that reflect the cosmopolitan idea of contemporary India. The rail line catering menu turns into a unique material that develops to take special care of the changing preferences and inclinations of a globalized world.

2. **Historical evolution of railway catering in India**

The verifiable advancement of railroad cooking in India is an entrancing excursion that reflects the development and improvement of the Indian Rail routes itself. The foundations of rail route catering can be followed back to the commencement of the rail line framework in the nineteenth hundred years, a period set apart by the presentation of the principal traveler prepares that associated various districts of English India.

During the early long stretches of railroad travel, providing food administrations were simple, with restricted choices accessible to travelers. The accentuation was on essential food, and tea slows down were among quick to show up at rail line stations. These shoddy slows down, frequently worked by nearby sellers, offered straightforward tidbits and the omnipresent cup of tea to fatigued explorers.

As the railroad network extended, so did the interest for more thorough cooking administrations. The frontier organization perceived the need to give better offices to travelers, prompting the foundation of the principal formal cooking administrations on Indian Railroads. By the late nineteenth 100 years, eating vehicles were presented on select trains, offering a more agreeable and formal feasting experience to travelers.

The feasting vehicles, described by rich insides and table help, denoted a huge jump forward in the development of railroad catering. Travelers could now partake in a formal dinner with a different menu that went past the essential tidbits presented at station slows down. The presentation of feasting vehicles improved the general travel insight as well as made way for the further advancement of railroad cooking in the years to come.

The right on time to mid-twentieth century saw a slow refinement and development of rail line catering administrations. The feasting vehicles developed to incorporate a more extensive scope of territorial and mainland dishes, taking care of the different preferences of travelers. The accentuation on quality and assortment turned out to be more articulated, and the railroad catering framework started to secure itself as an unmistakable part of train travel in India.

The post-freedom time achieved massive changes in the Indian Rail lines, and rail line providing food went through a change to fulfill the needs of a developing populace and a non-industrial country. The presentation of new trains, including express and superfast trains, required a redesign in cooking offices. The conventional feasting vehicles endured, however there was an acknowledgment of the requirement for more open and effective providing food administrations. To address this, portable cooking units were presented, considering the arrangement of dinners straightforwardly to travelers in their seats. This development denoted a takeoff from the proper setting of eating vehicles, giving a more helpful and time-effective answer for both short and significant distance ventures. The versatile cooking units laid the foundation for the cutting edge storage space vehicles that are vital to the rail line providing food framework today.

The 21st century acquired further progressions rail route catering, utilizing innovation to improve effectiveness and client experience. On the web and versatile based food requesting frameworks were presented, permitting travelers to pre-request feasts or browse a menu during their excursion. This innovative mix smoothed out the cooking system as well as extended the scope of culinary decisions accessible to travelers.

As of late, there has been a cognizant work to grandstand the rich and various culinary legacy of India through rail line providing food. Provincial fortes have found a noticeable put on the menu, offering travelers a sample of the nearby flavors as they navigate various states and domains. The culinary excursion has turned into a fundamental piece of the general travel insight, with the rail line providing food framework filling in as a culinary representative for the different and energetic cooking of India.

The calculated difficulties of working a portable kitchen on wheels have been met with development and commitment. Current storage space vehicles are furnished with best in class kitchens that stick to severe cleanliness and quality principles. Talented cooks work in these restricted spaces, guaranteeing that each dish is a demonstration of the culinary mastery that characterizes Indian food.

The rail route catering framework has likewise embraced the idea of supportability and mindful obtaining. Endeavors have been made to integrate privately obtained fixings, supporting provincial economies and diminishing the ecological effect of transportation. This shift towards manageable practices mirrors a more extensive consciousness of the significance of capable cooking with regards to an impacting world.

3. Significance of food in train travel

The meaning of food in train travel stretches out a long ways past simple food; a necessary perspective shapes the whole experience of the excursion. From the beginning of rail travel to the cutting edge time, food plays had a critical impact in making train ventures noteworthy, offering travelers a remarkable culinary odyssey as they cross different scenes.

One of the crucial components of this importance lies in the public part of feasting on trains. The common experience of partaking in a dinner with individual travelers encourages a feeling of brotherhood and local area. The cadenced ringing of utensils and the murmur of discussion in eating vehicles or among travelers in their seats make a climate that rises above the actual limits of the train. Outsiders become impermanent feasting colleagues, sharing stories and suggestions over a spread that joins them in the normal delight of good food.

Past the social angle, the meaning of food in train travel is profoundly entwined with the social embroidery of the areas navigated. Rail ventures in India, for instance, offer travelers a gastronomic visit through the country's different culinary legacy. Every locale contributes its extraordinary flavors and claims to fame, transforming the excursion into a tactile investigation of tastes and smells. The importance lies in the demonstration of eating as well as in the amazing chance to enjoy the quintessence of the different societies that make up the immense and shifted scene.

For some, the actual excursion is essentially as significant as the objective, and the meaning of food turns into a focal piece of this general insight. The eating vehicle, with its consistently changing perspectives outside the window, turns into a moving eatery that adds an additional layer of delight to the movement experience. Travelers can savor their dinners while watching scenes change — from clamoring urban communities to tranquil open country — making a powerful setting that upgrades the tactile delight of eating progressing.

The meaning of food in train travel additionally lies in the comfort it offers to travelers. With the coming of storage space vehicles and portable catering units, the times of conveying custom made dinners for long excursions have given way to the comfort of requesting a different scope of dishes on the train. Travelers can now browse a menu that takes care of their inclinations, whether it be local strengths, mainland cooking, or a straightforward cup of tea. This accommodation adds solace to the excursion as well as permits travelers to enjoy culinary encounters that may be unreasonable in different methods of transportation.

Besides, food fills in as a wellspring of solace and commonality in the transient climate of train travel. The smell of recognizable dishes and the flavor of solace food can summon a feeling of home and give comfort to travelers who may be a long way from their ordinary schedules. Along these lines, the meaning of food goes past the actual sustenance; it turns into a wellspring of profound prosperity, offering a feeling of dependability and association with the natural in the midst of the steadily changing landscape outside.

The meaning of food in train travel additionally mirrors the social and verifiable advancement of rail line cooking. From the early tea slows down and eating vehicles of the provincial period to the cutting edge, innovation driven cooking administrations, the advancement of rail route food reflects the more extensive changes in the public arena and travel propensities.

The consideration of local strengths and the accentuation on quality and assortment address a developing consciousness of the significance of giving travelers a balanced and fulfilling culinary experience.

As of late, as individuals have become more aware of their dietary options, the meaning of food in train make a trip has extended to incorporate contemplations of wellbeing and manageability. Railroad providing food administrations are progressively integrating choices for veggie lover and vegetarian counts calories, as well as privately obtained and natural fixings. This shift mirrors a more extensive cultural consciousness of the effect of food decisions on wellbeing and the climate, and the rail route cooking framework is adjusting to meet these developing assumptions.

The meaning of food in train travel is likewise highlighted by the recollections it makes. Numerous travelers affectionately review explicit feasts delighted in during their train processes, whether it's the quite hot samosas bought from a station merchant or the fragrant biryani relished in an eating vehicle. These culinary encounters become a vital piece of the story of the excursion, adding to an embroidery of recollections that get through lengthy after the train has arrived at its objective.

Chapter 1

The Spice Route

The Flavor Highway, a verifiable organization of shipping lanes that associated the East and West, is an enamoring part in the chronicles of human civilization. This multifaceted trap of pathways, both over land and ocean, worked with the trading of flavors, valuable stones, materials, and a horde of social impacts. The meaning of the Flavor Course goes a long ways past business; it was a channel for the blending of civilizations, an impetus for investigation, and a demonstration of the persevering through charm of extraordinary flavors that molded the course of history.

The starting points of the Flavor Course can be followed back to old times when flavors were not just culinary products but rather held significant social, strict, and restorative importance. In the good 'ol days, the Zest Course essentially connected the human advancements of the East — like China, India, and Southeast Asia — with those of the West, crossing areas from the Mediterranean to Europe. The appeal of flavors, including pepper, cinnamon, cloves, and nutmeg, charmed the creative mind of dealers, adventurers, and rulers the same.

One of the most eminent sections of the Flavor Course was the sea course that explored the Indian Sea. Indian shippers, adroit in nautical, set out on risky excursions across the Bedouin Ocean to exchange flavors with human advancements along the shores of the Persian Bay and the Red Ocean. This sea leg of the Flavor Course worked with exchange as well as turned into a conductor for the spread of social and strict thoughts, interfacing the different corners of the Indian Sea bowl.

The Silk Street, an old organization of shipping lanes that associated China with the Mediterranean, assumed a urgent part in the more extensive Flavor Course. While silk was a valued item traded along these courses, the Zest Course extended its extension to remember the rewarding exchange for flavors. Trains loaded down with merchandise navigated huge stretches of Focal Asia, crossing deserts and mountains to arrive at business sectors in the Center East and then some. This overland course turned into a mixture of societies, where thoughts, innovations, and merchandise streamed unreservedly, forming the improvement of social orders along its way.

India, with its rich embroidery of flavors, was a focal center point on the Zest Course. The antiquated ports of the Malabar Coast, like Calicut and Cochin, arose as clamoring focuses of exchange. Flavors like pepper, cardamom, and ginger from the rich scenes of Kerala found their direction into the holds of vendor ships, bound for distant terrains. Indian dealers, known for their navigational ability, cruised not just toward the west to the Center East and Europe yet additionally toward the east, arriving at the shores of Southeast Asia.

The sea Flavor Course arrived at its pinnacle during the middle age time frame, corresponding with the ascent of strong domains and marine countries. The Bedouin dealers, especially those from the Abbasid Caliphate, assumed an essential part in interfacing the East and West. Bedouin vendors went about as mediators, moving flavors from the Indian subcontinent to the business sectors of the Center East, where they were anxiously pursued for their culinary and restorative properties.

The archaic Zest Course saw the section of European powers into the field of flavor exchange. The craving to sidestep the Middle Easterner brokers and lay out direct shipping lanes with zest creating locales was a main impetus behind European investigation. In the late fifteenth hundred years, Portuguese wayfarers, drove by Vasco da Gama, effectively explored around the Cape of Good Expectation, opening an ocean course to India. This noticeable a huge change in the elements of the Zest Course, as European powers tried to lay out direct associations with flavor delivering locales, evading the customary land courses.

The opposition for command over flavor shipping lanes turned into a significant impulse for European investigation and colonization in the resulting hundreds of years. The Dutch, English, Spanish, and Portuguese competed for strength in the East Indies, laying out provinces and general stores to get their portion of the worthwhile zest exchange. The Moluccas, otherwise called the Zest Islands, turned into a point of convergence of conflict, as these islands were the essential wellspring of nutmeg and cloves.

The authentic meaning of the Flavor Course is indivisible from the mission for flavors that prodded investigation and molded the international scene. The zest exchange assumed a vital part the Time of Disclosure, impacting the journeys of Christopher Columbus, Ferdinand Magellan, and different pilgrims who tried to track down new courses to the flavor rich grounds of the East. The disclosure of the Americas, with their own wealth of flavors like bean stew peppers and vanilla, added new aspects to the worldwide zest exchange.

The Flavor Course was not just a channel for the development of products; it worked with a significant trade of social impacts. The Silk Street, specifically, was a mixture of civic establishments, where thoughts, innovations, and ways of thinking blended. The Bedouin researchers in the middle age Islamic world assumed a significant part in deciphering Greek and Roman texts, safeguarding and communicating old information that in the long run tracked down its manner back to Europe.

Along the sea Flavor Course, the blending of societies was apparent in the port urban communities that prospered as center points of exchange. Urban areas like Melaka in Southeast Asia and Calicut in India became cosmopolitan focuses where shippers, mariners, and researchers from various regions of the planet met. The mixing of customs, dialects, and religions in these port urban communities made a social union that improved the social orders along the Zest Course.

The Flavor Course likewise assumed a critical part in molding culinary practices all over the planet. Flavors, when considered extravagances open just to the world class, bit by bit turned out to be all the more generally accessible as shipping lanes extended. The imbuement of flavors into the foods of various districts changed culinary practices and made new flavor profiles. Pepper, for instance, turned into a pervasive flavoring in middle age European food, while cinnamon and cloves found their direction into sweet and exquisite dishes the same.

The effect of the Flavor Course on worldwide cooking styles is apparent even today. The culinary customs of Southeast Asia, with their dynamic utilization of flavors like lemongrass, galangal, and turmeric, bear the engraving of authentic exchange associations. In India, the unpredictable zest mixes of masalas and the utilization of flavors in Ayurvedic cooking are a demonstration of the getting through impact of the Flavor Course.

Essentially, the Mediterranean cooking styles, with their dependence on spices and flavors like oregano, thyme, and saffron, mirror the authentic associations along the Zest Course.

The Zest Course, while adding to social trade and monetary flourishing, additionally had its more obscure viewpoints. The opposition for command over zest delivering areas prompted clashes, colonization, and double-dealing. European powers, driven by the craving for imposing business model over the flavor exchange, participated in furious competitions that had extensive ramifications for the districts they looked to rule. The mission for flavors became interwoven with the more extensive account of dominion and the abuse of native populaces.

Regardless of the complicated history and the difficulties looked by the social orders along the Zest Course, the persevering through tradition of this verifiable organization is one of social variety and interconnectedness. The Zest Course was a channel for the trading of merchandise as well as thoughts, innovations, and creative articulations. The getting through allure of flavors, with their capacity to change everyday fixings into culinary joys, is a demonstration of the enduring effect of the Zest Course on worldwide preferences and cooking styles.

1.1 Exploration of diverse regional cuisines served on Indian trains

The investigation of different local cooking styles served on Indian trains is a culinary excursion that reflects the rich embroidery of India's social and gastronomic legacy. As trains cross the immense field of the subcontinent, the installed catering administrations become a powerful feature of the different provincial flavors that characterize the country. From the snow-covered pinnacles of the Himalayas to the waterfront stretches of Kerala, the culinary contributions on Indian trains present a variety of tastes that take special care of the changed palates of travelers.

In the northern areas of India, where the scene is overwhelmed by the rich fields of the Ganges, the cooking is described by powerful flavors and sweet-smelling flavors. The installed menu mirrors this with dishes like the notable North Indian biryanis, delicious kebabs, and rich margarine chicken. The fragrant smell of these dishes drifts through the train compartments, offering travelers a sample of the culinary legacy established in the verifiable and social customs of the locale.

As the train adventures toward the south, the culinary scene goes through a change. The installed menu presents the tart and coconut-mixed kinds of South Indian food. From the fiery Chettinad curries of Tamil Nadu to the tart rasam of Karnataka, the train turns into a gastronomic vessel shipping travelers through the different preferences of the southern states. The consistently present backup of dosas and idlis, presented with various chutneys and sambar, adds a soothing touch to the excursion.

Beach front districts contribute their own oceanic abundance to the rail line menu. New fish got from the Bedouin Ocean and Sound of Bengal tracks down its direction onto the plates of excited travelers. The unmistakable smell of fish curries from Kerala or the hot prawn masala from West Bengal adds a waterfront aspect to the culinary experience. The train turns into a course for travelers to relish the flavors that have supported seaside networks for ages.

Vegan delights, frequently eclipsed by their substantial partners, guarantee an unmistakable put on the railroad menu. Lentil-based dishes like Dal Tadka and Rajma Chawal feature the adaptability of vegan cooking in India. Every district confers its novel bend to these veggie lover works of art, bringing about a mixture of flavors that take special care of different preferences. The train venture turns into an investigation of the energetic and nutritious veggie lover choices that structure a necessary piece of Indian food.

The culinary investigation on Indian trains stretches out past the bounds of the storage space vehicle to nearby sellers at different stations. The stages change into outdoors advertises where travelers can enjoy road food fortes novel to every area. From the fiery chaat of Delhi to the appetizing vada pav of Mumbai, these extemporaneous experiences with neighborhood merchants add an additional layer of legitimacy to the culinary excursion. The train stations become waypoints for travelers to test the neighborhood road food seasons that characterize the culinary scene of the locale.

The meaning of territorial foods served on Indian trains lies in the different flavors as well as in the common feasting experience that unfurls inside the train compartments. The musical clunking of steel plates and the murmur of discussion make a vibe that rises above the simple demonstration of eating. Outsiders become feasting colleagues, sharing stories and proposals over a spread that joins them in the normal delight of good food. The train turns into a microcosm of India's social mosaic, where various people meet up through the common joy of fellowshipping together.

The rail line providing food experience isn't static; it develops to take special care of the changing preferences and inclinations of a dynamic and cosmopolitan culture. As India turns into a worldwide center, the culinary contributions on trains mirror a receptiveness to global flavors. Pasta, noodles, and mainland breakfast choices track down a spot close by conventional Indian toll, giving travelers a different exhibit of decisions that reflect the cosmopolitan idea of contemporary India. The train venture changes into a culinary experience that obliges a worldwide sense of taste.

The calculated difficulties of giving assorted territorial cooking styles on moving trains are met with inventiveness and devotion. The storeroom vehicle, furnished with best in class kitchens, works with accuracy to guarantee that each dish is a demonstration of the culinary skill that characterizes Indian cooking.

The gourmet specialists explore restricted spaces and time limitations to keep up with the quality and consistency of the contributions, transforming the moving train into a portable eatery that rivals fixed foundations in its culinary contributions.

As of late, the Indian Railroads has embraced innovation to upgrade the locally available feasting experience. On the web and versatile based food requesting frameworks permit travelers to pre-request dinners or look over a menu during their excursion. This innovative mix smoothes out the catering system as well as enables travelers with the adaptability to redo their culinary experience.

The investigation of different provincial cooking styles served on Indian trains rises above the utilitarian part of installed eating. It turns into a tactile and social excursion that unfurls with each passing mile. The train, with its consistently changing perspectives outside the window, turns into a versatile café that adds an additional layer of satisfaction to the movement experience. Travelers can appreciate local strengths, set out on off the cuff culinary experiences at station stages, and take part in public feasting that encourages associations among assorted people.

1.2 Influence of local flavors and spices on railway catering

The impact of neighborhood flavors and flavors on rail line catering in India is a culinary excursion that rises above simple food; it is a festival of the nation's rich and different gastronomic legacy. From the dynamic roads of Delhi to the seaside kitchens of Kerala, the consolidation of neighborhood fixings and flavors in rail route cooking makes a vivid encounter for travelers, mirroring the social embroidery of every area.

The groundwork of this culinary impact lies in the variety of Indian food, which is described by particular territorial flavors and a broad cluster of flavors. Flavors, frequently alluded to as the spirit of Indian cooking, are the central participants that loan profundity, smell, and intricacy to the heap dishes found the nation over. Every area flaunts its extraordinary flavor mix, exhibiting the topographical and social subtleties that shape the culinary scene.

In the northern locales of India, where the environment is helpful for the development of sweet-smelling flavors, the effect on railroad providing food is unquestionable. The vigorous and delightful dishes that exude from the storage space vehicles are injected with flavors like cumin, coriander, and mustard seeds. These flavors not just add an unmistakable fragrance to the sauces yet additionally add to the rich and generous person of North Indian food. Whether it's the notorious margarine chicken, the sweet-smelling biryanis, or the delicious kebabs, the embodiment of northern flavors penetrates the culinary contributions on trains.

As the train travels toward the south, the impact of neighborhood flavors takes a wonderful turn. The interesting kinds of tamarind, coconut, and curry leaves become noticeable in the dishes served ready. The storage room vehicles grandstand the variety of South Indian cooking with dishes like dosas, idlis, and a variety of chutneys. The tart tamarind-based curries of Tamil Nadu, the coconut-mixed indulgences of Kerala, and the flavor loaded arrangements of Andhra Pradesh add to a tactile excursion that reflects the one of a kind culinary marks of the southern states.

The waterfront stretches of India, where the ocean meets the land, add a sea impact to railroad catering. New fish, a staple of seaside food, tracks down its direction onto the plates of travelers. The particular fragrance of fish curries, prawn masalas, and crab arrangements mirrors the abundance of the Bedouin Ocean and Cove of Bengal. The flavors utilized in waterfront kitchens, for example, dark mustard seeds, fenugreek, and red bean stew, make an ensemble of flavors that grandstand the beach front culinary customs.

Vegan delights, impacted by the ripe fields and farming overflow of the nation, guarantee a conspicuous spot in rail line providing food menus. Lentils, beats, and a variety of vegetables structure the underpinning of veggie lover dishes served on trains. The impact of nearby flavors is clear in the readiness of dishes like Dal Tadka, Rajma Chawal, and different territorial varieties of vegetable curries. The different zest profiles utilized in vegan cooking add layers of intricacy to these dishes, making them a delightful and fulfilling part of the culinary excursion.

The meaning of nearby flavors and flavors in rail route cooking isn't restricted to the storage room vehicle alone; it stretches out to neighborhood merchants at different stations. These extemporaneous experiences with local road food sellers permit travelers to test the legitimate kinds of the area. From the zesty chaat of Delhi to the appetizing vada pav of Mumbai, these nearby claims to fame add an additional layer of validness to the culinary investigation. The rail line stations become gastronomic waypoints, offering travelers the valuable chance to enjoy the lively road food culture that characterizes every area.

The utilization of nearby flavors and flavors in rail line catering is likewise a demonstration of the versatility and genius of Indian Rail routes. The storeroom vehicle, working with accuracy and effectiveness, integrates district explicit fixings to make a different menu that takes care of the changing scenes and culinary inclinations of the excursion. The culinary specialists explore restricted spaces and calculated difficulties to guarantee that each dish is a genuine portrayal of the flavors related with the locales the train crosses.

Lately, there has been a cognizant work to exhibit the legitimacy of neighborhood flavors in rail line cooking. The accentuation on featuring local strengths and customary dishes mirrors an acknowledgment of the culinary variety that characterizes India. The mix of nearby fixings and flavors adds genuineness to the feasting experience as well as supports neighborhood economies and advances economical obtaining rehearses.

The impact of nearby flavors and flavors on railroad catering isn't static; it develops to take care of the changing preferences and inclinations of a dynamic and cosmopolitan culture. As India turns into a worldwide center, the culinary contributions on trains mirror a receptiveness to global flavors. Pasta, noodles, and mainland breakfast choices track down a spot close by conventional Indian toll, giving travelers a different cluster of decisions that reflect the cosmopolitan idea of contemporary India. The rail line catering framework turns into a powerful material that adjusts to the developing sense of taste of a globalized world.

The investigation of neighborhood flavors and flavors on trains isn't simply a gustatory encounter; a social excursion interfaces travelers with the rich legacy of the districts they cross. It goes past the demonstration of eating to turn into a tangible and vivid investigation of India's culinary mosaic. As the train twists through evolving scenes, the fragrances and flavors that consume the space become a sensorial guide, directing travelers through the different culinary practices that characterize every leg of the excursion.

1.3 Stories of iconic dishes from different regions

The culinary scene of India is an embroidery woven with accounts of notorious dishes that bear the engravings of history, culture, and local variety. From the northern fields toward the southern coast, every district contributes its remarkable flavors and culinary customs, making a lively mosaic of dishes that have become inseparable from the character of their separate regions.

In the northern areas of India, the notorious dish that rules is, in all honesty, the cherished "Spread Chicken." This rich and tasty curry has its starting points in the kitchens of Delhi, where it was made by Kundan Lal Gujral, the pioneer behind the renowned Moti Mahal eatery, during the 1950s. Rumors from far and wide suggest that the dish was conceived out of a craving to utilize the extra roasted chicken by stewing it in a tomato-based sauce improved with margarine and cream. The outcome was a culinary show-stopper that enraptured palates and before long turned into a staple in Delhi as well as the nation over. Spread Chicken, with its smooth surface and agreeable mix of flavors, has since turned into a representative of North Indian food, addressing the rich and liberal kinds of the area.

As one ventures southwards, the culinary scene goes through a change, and in the clamoring roads of Mumbai, the notorious "Vada Pav" becomes the overwhelming focus. This modest road food, frequently alluded to as the "Indian Burger," comprises of a flavored potato patty (vada) sandwiched between a pav (delicate bun) and liberally spread with chutneys. The starting points of Vada Pav can be followed back to Ashok Vaidya, a bite slow down proprietor in Dadar, Mumbai, who made this tasty and convenient nibble during the 1960s. What started as a reasonable and speedy feast for the middle class before long turned into an omnipresent road food, typifying the soul of Mumbai's quick moving life and various culinary impacts.

In the energetic kitchens of Kolkata, another notable dish arises — the "Kathi Roll." This road food delicacy has its underlying foundations in Nizam's, an unbelievable restaurant in Kolkata that was known for its kebabs. Rumors from far and wide suggest that during the 1930s, in a snapshot of culinary development, a kebab merchant chose to enclose the kebabs by a paratha, making a compact and scrumptious bite. The Kathi Roll, with its delicious fillings of flavored meats or paneer, enveloped by a delicate paratha, turned into a moment hit. Today, Kathi Rolls are a famous road food in Kolkata as well as tracked down their direction onto menus the nation over, addressing the combination of Mughlai flavors with nearby culinary customs.

Moving towards the western province of Gujarat, the famous "Dhokla" becomes the overwhelming focus. This steamed, light cake produced using matured rice and chickpea flour is a staple in Gujarati families. The starting points of Dhokla can be followed back to old times, however it acquired prominence as a morning meal or nibble thing in the twentieth hundred years. Dhokla's light and breezy surface, combined with the tart and gently flavored flavor, make it a darling dish in Gujarat as well as across India. It typifies the culinary ability of vegan Gujarati food and has turned into a solid and flexible tidbit delighted in by individuals, everything being equal.

As the train adventures toward the south towards the waterfront province of Kerala, the notorious "Kerala Sadya" turns into a culinary legend. Sadya is a customary dining experience served on a banana leaf during celebrations and festivities. It includes an intricate spread of vegan dishes, each overflowing with unmistakable flavors. The focal point of the Sadya is the sweet-smelling "Avial," a blended vegetable curry prepared with coconut and tempered with curry leaves. Rumors have spread far and wide suggesting that Avial was made by Bhima, one of the Pandava siblings from the Indian awe-inspiring Mahabharata. This notorious dish, with its mixture of vegetables and coconut-imbued sauce, encapsulates the culinary legacy of Kerala and is a fundamental piece of the social festivals in the locale.

Venturing towards the western province of Rajasthan, the notorious "Dal Baati Churma" arises as a culinary jewel. This generous and healthy dish is a blend of heated wheat-flour baatis (round bread), lentil dal, and sweet churma produced using coarsely ground wheat and jaggery.

The starting points of Dal Baati Churma can be followed back to the dry scenes of Rajasthan, where the shortage of water impacted the cooking strategies. The baatis are generally heated in the sand, giving them a novel and natural flavor. This famous dish mirrors the cleverness of Rajasthani cooking as well as represents the district's social and culinary wealth.

In the lively kitchens of Tamil Nadu, the notorious "Chettinad Chicken Curry" orders consideration. Known for its intense and searing flavors, Chettinad food has acquired recognition for its particular utilization of flavors. The Chettinad Chicken Curry, with its sweet-smelling mix of flavors like fennel, cloves, and peppercorns, embodies the vigorous and delightful nature of the area's culinary practices. Rumors have spread far and wide suggesting that the Chettiars, a trader local area from Chettinad, were known for their affection for flavors, which found their direction into the delightful dishes they made. This famous curry, with its intricate zest profile, has turned into a culinary representative of Chettinad cooking, exhibiting the district's culinary artfulness.

The impact of neighborhood flavors and flavors on famous dishes isn't restricted to explicit districts however is a string that winds through the texture of Indian food. The utilization of flavors, whether it's the cardamom-implanted treats of the north or the mustard seeds of the east, is a consistent idea that integrates the different culinary practices of the country. Each notorious dish recounts a story — of development, social impacts, and the well established association among food and personality.

In the clamoring roads of Old Delhi, the notorious "Paranthe Wali Gali" remains as a demonstration of the city's culinary heritage. This restricted path, fixed with shops work in stuffed paranthas (flatbreads), has been serving local people and guests the same for more than hundred years. The range of fillings, going from flavored potatoes to radish to curds, features the inventiveness and flexibility of Indian food. The Paranthe Wali Gali isn't simply a culinary objective; it is a living legacy site that typifies the soul of Old Delhi's gastronomic customs.

In the seaside city of Goa, the notorious "Fish Curry Rice" becomes the overwhelming focus. Impacted by Portuguese provincial history, Goan cooking is a wonderful combination of neighborhood flavors with worldwide impacts. The Fish Curry Rice, with its tart and coconut-mixed curry, is a staple in Goan families. The utilization of flavors like kokum, tamarind, and red chilies bestows a particular person to this dish, making it an image of Goa's energetic culinary character.

In the good countries of Himachal Pradesh, the famous "Sidu" catches the embodiment of mountain cooking. This steamed bread, loaded down with a combination of flavors, is a conventional dish delighted in by local people.

Sidu mirrors the genius of mountain networks, where the accessibility of fixings impacts the culinary manifestations. The glow of flavors and the good idea of Sidu make it an encouraging and notorious dish that resounds with the tough scenes of the Himalayas.

As the train ventures through the different territories of India, from the bone-dry deserts of Rajasthan to the lavish plant life of Assam, the accounts of notable dishes keep on unfurling. Every locale, with its extraordinary environment, soil, and social impacts, adds to the culinary kaleidoscope that characterizes Indian cooking. The famous dishes, established in history and custom, act as representatives of the locales they hail from, welcoming travelers on a culinary excursion that rises above topographical limits and catches the core of India's gastronomic legacy.

Chapter 2

The Culinary Engineers

The universe of gastronomy has seen a progressive development, with another type of culinary specialists arising as trailblazers in the domain of flavor, development, and method — these pioneers are suitably called "Culinary Designers." Dissimilar to conventional cooks who stick to laid out culinary standards, culinary architects embrace a multidisciplinary approach, blending science, innovation, and craftsmanship to make culinary encounters that push the limits of what is conceivable in the domain of food.

At the core of this development is a significant appreciation for the logical rules that oversee cooking. Culinary designers dive into the complexities of atomic gastronomy, applying logical techniques to comprehend the synthetic and actual cycles that happen during food arrangement. Strategies, for example, sous-vide cooking, spherification, and frothing become tests as well as essential devices in the culinary specialist's armory, permitting them to dismantle and remake flavors in uncommon ways.

One conspicuous figure in the domain of culinary designing is Ferran Adrià, the visionary gourmet expert behind the eminent eatery elBulli. Adrià's vanguard way to deal with gastronomy has procured him global recognition. At elBulli, he changed conventional fixings into startling structures, making dishes that obscured the lines among craftsmanship and food.

Through fastidious trial and error with surfaces, temperatures, and compound responses, Adrià reclassified the potential outcomes of flavor and show, making a permanent imprint on the culinary scene.

Culinary architects frequently saddle the force of innovation to hoist their manifestations. The reconciliation of state of the art gear, for example, sous-vide accuracy cookers, rotational evaporators, and axes, turns out to be natural in their kitchens. This mechanical ability stretches out past the simple demonstration of cooking; it impacts the whole eating experience. Computerized menus, intuitive introductions, and vivid eating ideas are all important for the culinary specialist's tool compartment to connect with coffee shops on a multisensory level.

Chasing culinary development, the job of fixings is raised to a fine art by culinary architects. Past the conventional storeroom staples, they investigate the undiscovered possibility of strange components. Fixings like agar, thickener, and fluid nitrogen become fundamental mediums through which culinary specialists shape their gastronomic dreams. The control of these fixings considers the production of palatable show-stoppers that overcome ordinary presumption.

Culinary specialists embrace the way of thinking that eating isn't just about food however a vivid excursion that connects every one of the faculties. Fragrances, surfaces, and visuals are cautiously arranged to bring out profound reactions and elevate the general feasting experience. The feasting table turns into a phase, and each dish a painstakingly created act in the culinary theater. This approach goes past the traditional idea of a dinner; it changes feasting into a fine art where each component, from plate show to the surrounding climate, adds to an all encompassing tactile experience.

In their quest for flawlessness, culinary architects frequently draw motivation from surprising sources. Cooperation with craftsmen, researchers, and planners turns into a characteristic expansion of their innovative strategy. The cross-fertilization of thoughts from different disciplines brings about culinary encounters that rise above the limits of customary kitchen rehearses. This cooperative methodology encourages a culture of steady learning and transformation, pushing the envelope of culinary inventiveness.

The expression "sub-atomic gastronomy" is frequently connected with crafted by culinary specialists. Authored by physicist Nicholas Kurti and scientist Hervé This during the 1980s, sub-atomic gastronomy alludes to the logical investigation of the physical and compound cycles that happen during cooking. Culinary designers have embraced this methodology, involving it as an establishment to try different things with the change of fixings on a sub-atomic level. By understanding the logical standards at play, they can make dishes that challenge assumptions and rethink culinary standards.

Acclaimed gourmet specialist Heston Blumenthal is one more illuminator in the domain of culinary designing. His eatery, The Fat Duck, flaunts a menu that peruses like a logical examination, highlighting dishes like "Sound of the Ocean," where coffee shops are given an iPod playing sea sounds to improve the fish insight. Blumenthal's investigation of multisensory eating has prompted a reconsidering of conventional English cooking, injecting it with a feeling of eccentricity and development.

The culinary architect's journey for advancement isn't bound to very good quality gastronomy; it stretches out to the domain of maintainability and food availability. Developments in plant-based cooking, elective proteins, and supportable obtaining are fundamental parts of their culinary way of thinking. Culinary specialists perceive the obligation to address worldwide difficulties, for example, environmental change and food security. Through imaginative strategies and innovative reasoning, they add to the development of a more maintainable and evenhanded food industry.

Culinary designing has tracked down its direction into culinary instruction, with establishments integrating logical standards and present day procedures into their educational plan. Hopeful cooks are not generally bound to customary culinary preparation however are urged to investigate the convergence of science and gastronomy. This change in training mirrors the business' affirmation of the significance of keeping up to date with mechanical headways and logical revelations.

While the expression "Culinary Architect" might be moderately new, the soul of culinary development has profound authentic roots. Visionaries like Marie-Antoine Carême and Auguste Escoffier established the groundworks for current gastronomy by classifying culinary methods and laying out the traditional French kitchen. Culinary designers expand upon this heritage, embracing the apparatuses and information accessible to them in the 21st 100 years to push the limits of what is conceivable in the culinary domain.

The impact of culinary designing reaches out past the kitchen and into the domain of food business venture. New businesses and food tech organizations drove by culinary designers are upsetting customary food creation and circulation models. From 3D-printed food varieties to lab-developed meats, these pioneers are molding the fate of how we produce and devour food. The crossing point of culinary masterfulness and innovation is leading to another time in gastronomy, where the limits between the kitchen and the lab obscure.

2.1 Behind-the-scenes look at the chefs and kitchen staff responsible for railway catering

Behind the buzzing about of the rail route venture, there exists a world inside, where the masterfulness of rail route catering shows some signs of life. This in the background domain is an ensemble of coordination, accuracy, and culinary craftsmanship, organized by a committed group of gourmet specialists and kitchen staff working vigorously to guarantee that travelers experience a magnificent culinary excursion.

The foundation of rail route catering is the kitchen staff, a different gathering of people who by and large structure the motor that drives the culinary experience on trains. From gifted culinary specialists to fastidious kitchen colleagues, this group assumes a urgent part in changing the storage room vehicle into a versatile kitchen, where the wizardry of flavors unfurls in the midst of the musical bang of wheels on tracks.

In charge of this culinary endeavor are the cooks, frequently overlooked yet truly great individuals who carry their culinary ability to the bound spaces of the storage room vehicle. Prepared in the specialty of performing multiple tasks, these gourmet experts explore the difficulties of a moving train with artfulness, guaranteeing that each dish is a demonstration of their culinary ability. From the fragrant curries of the north to the coconut-injected luxuries of the south, cooks tailor their abilities to take care of the different local inclinations of travelers.

The coordinated operations of cooking on a moving train present extraordinary difficulties that request an elevated degree of flexibility and expertise. Gourmet specialists should figure the requirements of room, the restricted accessibility of fixings, and the need to keep up with quality during the excursion. The storage space vehicle changes into a unique work area where cooks deftly balance the accuracy of their culinary strategies with the imperatives of the railroad climate.

The menu arranging process is a cooperative exertion that includes the cooks as well as nutritionists, food handling specialists, and calculated organizers. The test lies in organizing a menu that takes care of different palates while sticking to the limitations of room, stockpiling, and transportation. The cooks' inventiveness is scrutinized as they plan a menu that mirrors the culinary variety of the locales the train crosses.

The storage room vehicle itself is an efficient space, much the same as a smaller and portable café kitchen. Each square inch is improved for proficiency, with capacity regions carefully organized to oblige the fixings, utensils, and gear required for the excursion. The culinary experts work with military accuracy, boosting the utilization of accessible assets without settling for less on the nature of the dishes.

Kitchen collaborators, the unrecognized yet truly great individuals of railroad catering, structure the foundation of the activity. Liable for errands going from fixing planning to dish plating, these people work pair with the gourmet experts to guarantee the consistent execution of every dinner. Their jobs require a mix of culinary expertise, speed, and flexibility as they travel through the reduced kitchen, expecting the necessities of the gourmet specialists and keeping a consistent work process.

The difficulties looked by the kitchen staff reach out past the specialized parts of cooking. The unique idea of rail line make a trip requests consistent transformation to factors like changing weather patterns, postponements, and varieties in the accessibility of fixings at various stops. This requires a degree of strength and critical ability to think that goes past the conventional kitchen climate.

Sanitation is vital in railroad cooking, and the kitchen staff goes through thorough preparation to stick to severe cleanliness norms. From the obtaining of fixings to the capacity and arrangement of dinners, each step is painstakingly checked to guarantee the security and prosperity of travelers. The kitchen staff works with the comprehension that every feast served on the train isn't simply food yet an indispensable piece of the general travel insight.

The kinship among the kitchen staff is an essential component in keeping up with the proficiency and spirit of the group. The lacking elbow room of the storage space vehicle cultivate a feeling of collaboration and common help, where every part assumes an essential part in the aggregate progress of the activity. The quick moving climate requests clear correspondence and synchronization, transforming the storage space vehicle into a culinary gathering where each part adds to the orchestra of flavors.

While the travelers partake in the their rewards for so much hard work, the kitchen staff frequently stays concealed, working in the background to guarantee a consistent eating experience. The fulfillment got from realizing that their culinary manifestations add to the delight of travelers turns into the main thrust for these culinary experts.

The kitchen staff's commitment isn't only a task; it is an energy for making essential feasting encounters in the midst of the unique setting of train travel.

The railroad catering venture stretches out past the storage room vehicle and into nearby business sectors and merchants at different stations. The kitchen staff teams up with neighborhood providers to source new fixings, adding a bona fide touch to the provincial flavors served on the train. This cooperation upholds nearby economies as well as guarantees an association between the railroad catering activity and the culinary customs of the districts navigated.

Lately, innovative progressions have impacted railroad catering, smoothing out processes and upgrading the general insight. On the web and versatile based food requesting frameworks permit travelers to pre-request feasts, redo their inclinations, and browse a different menu during their excursion. This combination of innovation improves traveler comfort as well as adds a layer of effectiveness to the kitchen staff's tasks.

In spite of the difficulties and limitations, the kitchen staff's obligation to conveying quality dinners on a moving train embodies the soul of culinary craftsmanship. Their capacity to adjust, enhance, and team up reflects their culinary abilities as well as their energy for making a paramount eating experience in the midst of the one of a kind scenery of railroad travel.

2.2 Training and challenges faced in providing quality meals at scale

The arrangement of value feasts at scale in rail line cooking is a perplexing and complex cycle that includes thorough preparation and a sharp comprehension of the provokes remarkable to the climate of a moving train. The people engaged with this try go through particular preparation to furnish them with the abilities, information, and versatility expected to convey culinary greatness for a huge scope.

Preparing for rail route catering staff starts with an emphasis on the essentials of culinary expressions. Culinary specialists and kitchen aides go through proper schooling in cooking strategies, menu arranging, and sanitation guidelines. This fundamental preparation guarantees that the kitchen staff has the fundamental abilities expected to make a different and tasty menu that takes care of the shifted inclinations of travelers.

A vital part of preparing in rail route catering is the accentuation on flexibility. The powerful idea of train travel presents difficulties that are not experienced in conventional café kitchens. The moving climate, restricted space, and shifting circumstances during the excursion require a novel arrangement of abilities. Gourmet specialists and kitchen collaborators go through recreations and functional activities to look into the difficulties of cooking on a moving train, guaranteeing that they can keep up with quality and proficiency regardless of the limitations.

The kitchen staff is prepared to deal with the strategies of fixing obtaining and the board. Given the restricted extra room accessible in the storeroom vehicle, successful stock administration becomes basic. Preparing programs center around enhancing stockpiling, limiting waste, and guaranteeing that fixings stay new all through the excursion. The kitchen staff figures out how to team up with neighborhood providers at various stations, adding a provincial touch to the feasts by obtaining new and bona fide fixings.

Sanitation is a central worry in railroad catering, and preparing programs focus on this viewpoint. Kitchen staff go through intensive training on cleanliness practices, sterilization, and safe food dealing with. The objective is to ingrain a culture of neatness and obligation, perceiving that the wellbeing and prosperity of travelers rely upon the severe adherence to sanitation norms.

Correspondence and cooperation are fundamental parts of preparing in rail line cooking. The crowdedness of the storage room vehicle request viable correspondence among the kitchen staff. Colleagues figure out how to facilitate flawlessly, guaranteeing a smooth work process even in the speedy and restricted space. This cooperative soul is encouraged through preparing activities and recreations that mirror this present reality challenges looked during a train venture.

Past the specialized parts of cooking, preparing programs in rail line catering frequently remember modules for client assistance. The kitchen staff is taught on the significance of making a positive feasting experience for travelers. This includes planning delectable feasts as well as drawing in with travelers in a cordial and expert way. The objective is to change the demonstration of feasting on a train into a vital and charming experience.

Challenges in giving quality dinners at scale in rail route cooking are complex. One of the essential difficulties is the restriction of room. The storage space vehicle, however outfitted with best in class offices, is innately conservative. Cooks and kitchen partners should move proficiently inside this bound space, expecting them to excel at association and coordination. Every last trace of the kitchen is improved to oblige fixings, hardware, and the culinary group, requesting accuracy and effectiveness in each development.

The moving idea of train travel adds an additional layer of intricacy to the culinary interaction. The gourmet experts and kitchen aides should adjust to the steady movement, guaranteeing that cooking procedures, fixing taking care of, and plating can be executed immaculately regardless of the train's development. This challenge requires an elevated degree of expertise and versatility, which is sharpened through preparing practices that mimic the states of a moving train.

One more huge test is the fluctuation in conditions at various stations. The kitchen staff should be ready to work with the fixings accessible at each quit, adjusting the menu in light of local claims to fame and occasional contributions. This requires a profound comprehension of the culinary customs of different locales, and the capacity to make an agreeable mix of flavors that mirrors the geological variety navigated by the train.

Strategic difficulties in obtaining fixings and keeping up with newness add one more layer of intricacy. The kitchen staff should facilitate with nearby providers at each station, guaranteeing a consistent store network that upholds the ceaseless arrangement of new and excellent fixings.

The fluctuation in neighborhood markets and accessibility of explicit things present consistent difficulties that require speedy reasoning and versatility.

Weather patterns likewise assume a part in the difficulties looked by rail route cooking staff. Outrageous temperatures, mugginess, and other climate related elements can affect fixing capacity, cooking cycles, and in general kitchen effectiveness. Preparing programs frequently remember modules for dealing with these natural difficulties to guarantee that the kitchen staff is prepared to deal with any circumstances experienced during the excursion.

In spite of the difficulties, the kitchen staff in rail line providing food is driven by a promise to conveying quality dinners at scale. The deep satisfaction in giving a vital feasting experience to travelers fills their devotion to beating deterrents and persistently working on their abilities. The preparation got turns into an establishment for development, versatility, and the quest for culinary greatness in the consistently developing scene of railroad catering.

2.3 Innovation in menu planning and food preparation

In the domain of rail route cooking, development in menu arranging and food readiness is a powerful power that continually advances to meet the different and knowing preferences of travelers. The culinary scene on board prepares has seen a change in perspective, driven by a pledge to meet as well as surpass the assumptions for voyagers. From the cautious curation of menus to the reception of state of the art cooking procedures, advancement is at the front of changing the feasting experience on trains.

Menu arranging, a pivotal part of rail line providing food, has gone through an upset because of the interest for different and great culinary contributions. Conventional train admission, frequently condemned for its tedium and staleness, has given approach to nicely organized menus that mirror the culinary variety of the districts navigated by the train. Railroad catering administrations presently focus on the incorporation of local strengths, guaranteeing that travelers leave on a culinary excursion that reflects the geological embroidery outside their windows.

The impact of neighborhood flavors is a vital component in creative menu arranging. Culinary experts working in rail line cooking team up with nearby providers at different stations to source new and genuine fixings. This imbuement of territorial produce not just adds a component of genuineness to the feasts yet in addition upholds nearby economies. The menus become dynamic, adjusting to the changing scenes and culinary customs experienced during the excursion.

The reconciliation of innovation plays had a significant impact in upsetting menu arranging in rail line cooking. On the web and versatile based food requesting frameworks permit travelers to get to menus, tweak their inclinations, and pre-request dinners. This mechanical development improves traveler comfort, giving them a different exhibit of decisions and guaranteeing that their culinary inclinations are taken care of during the excursion.

Unique dietary prerequisites and inclinations are given cautious thought in creative menu arranging. Rail line providing food administrations perceive the significance of obliging assorted dietary necessities, including veggie lover, vegetarian, without gluten, and other particular choices. This comprehensive methodology guarantees that each traveler, no matter what their dietary limitations, can partake in a delightful and tasty eating experience ready.

The idea of irregularity is embraced in imaginative menu arranging, adjusting the contributions to the accessibility of new, occasional fixings. This not just upgrades the flavor and nature of the dishes yet additionally adds to a supportable and eco-accommodating methodology. The accentuation on irregularity guarantees that travelers are blessed to receive the best of nearby produce during their excursion.

Notwithstanding customary charge, rail route cooking administrations have extended their menus to incorporate a combination of worldwide foods. Travelers can now appreciate global flavors, going from mainland breakfast choices to pasta dishes and Asian-motivated feasts. This imbuement of worldwide impacts mirrors the cosmopolitan idea of train travel and takes special care of the assorted culinary inclinations of travelers.

The idea of live cooking stations is one more imaginative methodology embraced in railroad providing food. A few trains highlight gourmet specialists who set up specific dishes before travelers, giving a live culinary encounter. This not just adds a component of amusement to the eating system yet in addition permits travelers to observe the newness and ability engaged with setting up their feasts.

Food show is raised to an artistic expression in creative menu arranging. The visual allure of dishes is painstakingly thought of, changing every dinner into a banquet for the eyes. Innovative plating strategies, imaginative embellishments, and tender loving care add to a feasting experience that connects every one of the faculties. The feel of the feasting experience are indispensable to making an important excursion for travelers.

Past menu arranging, advancement stretches out to food readiness methods in rail line catering. Customary strategies are supplemented by current culinary innovations, for example, sous-vide cooking, acceptance warming, and vacuum-fixing. These strategies guarantee that the quality and kind of the dishes are kept up with, even in the difficult states of a moving train.

Sous-vide cooking, specifically, has acquired prominence in railroad catering for its capacity to save the surface and dampness of fixings. This technique includes vacuum-fixing food in plastic and slow-cooking it in a water shower at an exact temperature. The outcome is delicate, tasty dishes that are cooked flawlessly, no matter what the difficulties presented via train travel.

Creative cooking procedures likewise incorporate the utilization of enlistment warming in storage space vehicles. Enlistment cookers give exact command over temperature, empowering culinary experts to cook effectively and keep up with the honesty of fixings. The reception of these cutting edge innovations upgrades the general productivity of food planning on trains.

Endeavors to limit squander and advance supportability are incorporated into imaginative food planning rehearses. Kitchen staff go through preparing on upgrading fixing utilization, decreasing abundance bundling, and executing eco-accommodating practices. These drives line up with more extensive worldwide worries about ecological effect and add to a more capable way to deal with rail line catering.

Challenges in food readiness on trains, like restricted space and fluctuating ecological circumstances, require an imaginative and versatile mentality. Culinary specialists and kitchen staff are prepared to investigate and track down inventive answers for unexpected snags. The capacity to make do and develop turns into an important range of abilities, guaranteeing that the culinary excursion stays continuous in spite of the difficulties presented by the exceptional setting of a moving train.

Chapter 3

Menu Classics

In the always developing scene of culinary encounters, certain dishes go the distance, procuring the regarded title of "Menu Works of art." These are the ageless manifestations that have risen above patterns and crazes, becoming darling staples that elegance menus across the globe. From the debauched guilty pleasure of an impeccably cooked steak to the soothing straightforwardness of an exemplary pasta dish, these menu works of art are not just things on a menu; they are symbols that bring out a feeling of sentimentality, custom, and culinary dominance.

One such exemplary that orders a lasting presence on menus overall is the respected Caesar Salad. Imagined in Tijuana, Mexico, by Caesar Cardini during the 1920s, this salad has turned into an image of fresh newness and strong flavors. Romaine lettuce leaves are gently covered in a lively dressing produced using garlic, anchovies, olive oil, and parmesan cheddar, then finished off with crunchy bread garnishes. The Caesar Salad is a demonstration of the immortal allure of straightforwardness and equilibrium in culinary manifestations.

The charm of an impeccably cooked steak has made it an undisputed exemplary on menus from steakhouses to high end foundations. Whether it's a delicious Filet Mignon, a powerful Ribeye, or a delightful New York Strip, the specialty of barbecuing or singing a steak flawlessly has been sharpened to culinary flawlessness. Joined by exemplary sides like pureed potatoes or a variety of occasional vegetables, a top notch steak stays a festival of savage extravagance.

Pasta, in its horde structures, has cut a super durable spot in the hearts and palates of cafes around the world. The Spaghetti Bolognese, a quintessential Italian dish, includes a rich and exquisite meat sauce injected with tomatoes, garlic, onions, and a variety of sweet-smelling spices. The still somewhat firm flawlessness of the pasta joined with the generous kinds of the sauce has made this exemplary a soothing most loved that rises above social limits.

Encapsulating the quintessence of French culinary masterfulness, Coq au Vin is an exemplary that hails from the Burgundy district. This dish raises humble fixings —

chicken, red wine, mushrooms, and pearl onions — into an ensemble of flavors. Slow-cooked flawlessly, the delicate chicken retains the profound, nuanced notes of the red wine, making a dish that typifies the respected French practice of changing straightforward fixings into culinary magnum opuses.

The captivating smell of garlic, olive oil, and tomatoes penetrates the air when a plate of Pasta Pomodoro is introduced. This Italian exemplary praises the splendor of straightforwardness, highlighting ready tomatoes, garlic, and new basil threw with still somewhat firm pasta. The marriage of flavors in Pasta Pomodoro is a demonstration of the specialty of creating simple dishes that permit every fixing to sparkle.

The immortal allure of the unassuming Burger has made it a worldwide sensation. From road merchants to connoisseur foundations, the exemplary mix of a very much prepared meat patty, new lettuce, delicious tomato, and a dab of tart ketchup and mustard rises above social and culinary limits. The Burger's flexibility has led to vast varieties, each adding to its getting through ubiquity.

In the domain of fish, the exemplary Bouillabaisse from the port city of Marseille becomes the overwhelming focus. This good angler's stew exhibits a variety of fish — from fish and shellfish to sweet-smelling spices and flavors — all stewed together to make a rich and tasty stock. Presented with a side of rouille, a garlic-injected mayonnaise, Bouillabaisse is a festival of the bounties of the ocean.

The marriage of bread, cheddar, and spread leads to the famous Croque Monsieur, a darling French sandwich. Layers of ham and Gruyère cheddar are sandwiched between cuts of dried up bread, then, at that point, slathered with béchamel sauce prior to being heated to brilliant flawlessness. The outcome is a consoling and liberal exemplary that has turned into an image of relaxed polish in French cooking.

A culinary excursion through exemplary menus wouldn't be finished without the notice of the immortal Tiramisu. This Italian pastry, with layers of espresso doused ladyfingers and mascarpone cheddar, cleaned with cocoa powder, is an ensemble of surfaces and flavors. Tiramisu's choice harmony between pleasantness and lavishness has made it an installation on dessert menus around the world, catching the hearts of those with an inclination for the heavenly.

The quintessential French Onion Soup, with its profound, caramelized flavors and gooey dissolved cheddar besting, has gotten its put as an exemplary starter on menus. This good soup, generally made with caramelized onions, hamburger stock, and a fresh cut of loaf finished off with softened Gruyère cheddar, is a consoling preface to a paramount eating experience.

The persevering through allure of the Margherita Pizza lies in its effortlessness and the nature of its fixings. With a slight outside layer, tart pureed tomatoes, new mozzarella cheddar, and a dispersing of basil leaves, the Margherita Pizza embodies the specialty of allowing a couple of key parts to sparkle. An exemplary has turned into a material for incalculable varieties, yet the first remaining parts an immortal #1.

The Egg Benedict, with its impeccably poached eggs settled on Canadian bacon and a toasted English biscuit, hung in smooth hollandaise sauce, is an early lunch exemplary that has endured for an extremely long period. The fragile harmony between surfaces and flavors in this dish has made it a staple on breakfast and early lunch menus, offering a sumptuous beginning to the day.

An exemplary that overcomes any barrier between solace food and culinary artfulness is the Chicken Pot Pie. With its flaky outside layer, rich filling of chicken, vegetables, and a flavorful sauce, the Chicken Pot Pie is the encapsulation of homestyle cooking raised to connoisseur levels. Its nostalgic appeal and fulfilling flavors make it a loved exemplary that rises above ages.

The universe of treats invites the immortal Fruity dessert, a soothing cut of History of the U.S. With its rich, flaky outside layer supporting delicate cuts of cinnamon-flavored apples, the Fruity dessert epitomizes the glow and custom of home-prepared goodness. Whether delighted in the current style or all alone, the Fruity dessert stays an exemplary pastry that resounds with the straightforward delights of life.

The exemplary Margarita mixed drink, with its ideal mix of tequila, triple sec, and lime juice served over ice, exemplifies the craft of mixology. This notorious mixed drink, with its invigorating citrusy notes and a touch of salt, has turned into an image of recreation and festivity, gracing mixed drink menus all over the planet.

The getting through prominence of exemplary dishes lies in their capacity to bring out a feeling of commonality and immortality. As culinary patterns travel every which way, these menu works of art stay enduring, offering a soothing shelter for those looking for the recognizable hug of custom. From the unassuming starting points of territorial fortes to the worldwide acknowledgment they appreciate today, these works of art keep on captivating cafes, advising us that, in the realm of culinary pleasures, a few flavors are genuinely immortal.

3.1 Examination of timeless and popular dishes on railway menus

The culinary excursion on trains rises above simple transportation; it unfurls as an ensemble of flavors that enthrall travelers from different foundations. In the midst of the cadenced murmur of wheels on tracks, railroad menus grandstand an organized determination of immortal and well known dishes that have become meaningful of the movement experience. These culinary contributions satisfy hunger as well as weave a story of social extravagance, local variety, and culinary masterfulness.

One of the persevering through works of art that graces railroad menus across the globe is the Chicken Curry. This dish, with its foundations in different culinary customs, exemplifies an agreeable combination of flavors. Whether propelled by the fragrant flavors of Indian food, the coconut-mixed curries of Southeast Asia, or the exquisite lavishness of European varieties, Chicken Curry has turned into an image of culinary all inclusiveness on rail route ventures. Its presence on menus mirrors a sign of approval for the soothing and vigorous nature of this immortal dish.

The humble however all around adored Sandwich is one more robust on railroad menus. With its adaptability, comfort, and vast varieties, the sandwich takes special care of different preferences and dietary inclinations. From the exemplary Club Sandwich with layers of turkey, bacon, lettuce, and tomato to vegan choices like the Caprese or Veggie Enjoyment, sandwiches offer a compact and fulfilling feasting answer for travelers moving. The getting through allure of the sandwich lies in its capacity to take special care of both straightforwardness and connoisseur development.

A quintessential component of rail route menus is the notorious Chicken Sandwich, a group pleaser that rises above social limits. Containing delicious chicken, fresh lettuce, succulent tomatoes, and mayonnaise or an exquisite sauce, the Chicken Sandwich is an ideal encapsulation of the marriage among comfort and flavor. Its notoriety originates from its versatility to different local impacts, guaranteeing that travelers from various areas of the planet can track down solace in this natural yet different contribution.

As the train navigates various districts, the menu frequently gives proper respect to nearby culinary customs, exhibiting provincial strengths that commend the different kinds of the excursion. In India, the railroad menu could highlight the consistently famous Biryani, a fragrant and delightful rice dish mixed with flavors and loaded down with delicious bits of meat or vegetables. Biryani, with its rich history and territorial varieties, is a culinary minister that acquaints travelers with the lively embroidery of Indian food.

The persevering through allure of Pasta dishes has likewise tracked down its put on railroad menus, giving an encouraging and recognizable choice for travelers. Works of art like Spaghetti Bolognese, with its generous meat sauce, or Pasta Pomodoro, including tomatoes, garlic, and basil, exhibit the widespread love for Italian cooking. The straightforwardness and flexibility of pasta settle on it a go-to decision for those looking for a generous and fulfilling feast on their rail process.

In the domain of solace food, the Barbecued Cheddar Sandwich remains as a reference point of effortlessness and extravagance. Its appeal lies in the ideal association of gooey liquefied cheddar between cuts of rich, toasted bread. This exemplary dish, frequently joined by a side of tomato soup, summons a feeling of wistfulness and home-style solace that reverberates with travelers on their excursions.

Veggie lover contributions on rail line menus take care of a different scope of dietary inclinations and social decisions. The Vegetable Curry, enlivened by the rich practices of vegan food, exhibits a variety of vegetables washed in sweet-smelling flavors and presented with rice or bread. This veggie lover exemplary not just fulfills the palates of the people who follow a sans meat diet yet in addition praises the culinary imagination that can be accomplished without the requirement for creature items.

The notorious Railroad Lamb Curry, with its beginnings well established throughout the entire existence of train travel in India, is a dish that mirrors the social meaning of rail route cooking. This tasty and generous curry, frequently presented with rice or bread, gives proper respect to the culinary legacy of rail line eating. Its presence on present day menus associates travelers with the sentimentality of former periods while railroad eating was an occasion to be relished.

Fish contributions on rail route menus catch the substance of waterfront areas, carrying the kinds of the ocean to travelers on their excursions. The immortal Fried fish and French fries, an English work of art, is a staple that has found its direction onto rail route menus, offering a fresh and fulfilling dish that resounds with those looking for a sample of oceanic extravagance. This dish, with its brilliant brown battered fish and going with fries, has turned into a solace food symbol.

An assessment of ageless and well known dishes on rail route menus would be fragmented without the notice of the consistently famous Breakfast contributions. The Full English Breakfast, with its gathering of eggs, bacon, hotdog, tomatoes, and toast, typifies the generous and fulfilling start to the day that travelers look for. This exemplary breakfast spread isn't simply a dinner; a ceremonial signals the start of another day, a culinary practice that rises above social limits.

For those with a sweet tooth, rail route menus frequently highlight immortal Pastries that add a bit of guilty pleasure to the excursion. The exemplary Chocolate Cake, with its rich and damp layers, or the immortal Fruity dessert, with its flaky hull and flavored apple filling, are treats that inspire a feeling of festivity. These treats, frequently presented with a bit of cream or a scoop of vanilla frozen yogurt, give a sweet finale to the culinary excursion on trains.

In the realm of refreshments, the persevering through prominence of the Chai, or tea, couldn't possibly be more significant. A staple on rail route menus in nations like India, Chai is something other than a drink; it is a social peculiarity. The fragrant mix of flavors, tea leaves, and milk in Chai reverberates with travelers, offering an encouraging and reviving experience during their excursion.

Espresso, with its rich fragrance and stimulating properties, is another immortal drink that graces railroad menus around the world. Whether it's a basic cup of dark espresso or a more intricate Cappuccino or Latte, the presence of espresso on rail route menus mirrors the all inclusive appreciation for this stimulated pleasure. The custom of partaking in some espresso while looking out at the passing scenes has turned into a basic piece of the train travel insight.

As railroad menus keep on developing, there is a developing accentuation on taking care of different dietary inclinations and wellbeing cognizant decisions. Veggie lover and vegetarian choices have become more conspicuous, offering a scope of delightful and nutritious decisions for travelers looking for plant-based other options. The joining of plates of mixed greens, new organic products, and lighter dinner choices mirrors a more extensive familiarity with wellbeing and dietary variety in present day rail line catering.

3.2 Evolution of menu choices over the years

The development of menu decisions throughout the long term in the domain of railroad cooking is a dazzling excursion that reflects the evolving tastes, culinary patterns, and social changes in the public eye. From the beginning of utilitarian eating on trains to the current period of connoisseur encounters, the change of menu decisions mirrors a unique exchange of development, globalization, and a profound comprehension of travelers' different inclinations.

In the beginning long periods of rail route travel, menu decisions were simple and even minded. The emphasis was on giving food to travelers during their excursions instead of making a paramount feasting experience. Straightforward, generous choices like stews, sandwiches, and tough bread ruled early railroad menus. The accentuation was on reasonableness, with a plan to offer dinners that could endure the difficulties of movement, including restricted capacity and fluctuating circumstances.

As rail travel developed and turned out to be more available, so did the assumptions for travelers. The mid-twentieth century saw a shift towards offering a more different and refined determination of menu decisions. Eating vehicles arose as spaces where travelers could partake in a relaxed feast with a climate likened to a café. Exemplary dishes, for example, Broil Meat, Chicken à la Lord, and Lobster Newberg became staples on upscale train menus, giving a dash of polish to the movement experience.

The appearance of worldwide train travel additionally widened the skylines of menu decisions. Trains crossing borders became culinary diplomats, acquainting travelers with an embroidery of worldwide flavors. The Orient Express, for instance, embodied extravagance train travel with its menus highlighting a combination of European foods. The eating vehicles of these notorious trains became stages for culinary vain behaviors, displaying the best dishes from different areas.

The mid-twentieth century likewise saw the presentation of pre-bundled and comfort food varieties on trains. The ascent of cheap food culture affected rail route cooking, prompting the incorporation of things like burgers, wieners, and pre-bundled sandwiches on menus. This shift took special care of the rising interest for fast and helpful feast choices, particularly as train make a trip extended to oblige a more extensive segment of travelers.

In any case, by the late twentieth 100 years and into the 21st 100 years, there was a noticeable change in the way of thinking of rail route providing food. A developing accentuation on quality, assortment, and culinary development arose, driven by an advancing food culture and uplifted customer assumptions. Rail line organizations started teaming up with famous gourmet specialists to plan menus that reflected both neighborhood and global culinary patterns.

The globalization of food culture altogether impacted the advancement of menu decisions on trains. Travelers started to look for a more different and connoisseur eating experience, provoking railroad cooking administrations to present a more extensive cluster of worldwide dishes. Menus began including choices propelled by Asian, Center Eastern, and South American foods, mirroring a craving for culinary investigation during the excursion.

A remarkable pattern lately is the rising spotlight on wellbeing cognizant menu decisions. Travelers, more receptive to dietary inclinations and wholesome contemplations, started looking for lighter, plant-based, and sans gluten choices. Railroad catering answered by consolidating servings of mixed greens, veggie lover dishes, and better snacks into their menus, lining up with the developing attention to wellbeing and careful eating.

Mechanical progressions likewise assumed a part in molding menu decisions on trains. The presentation of locally available kitchens furnished with current apparatuses considered more modern cooking procedures. This innovative mix empowered culinary experts to set up a more extensive scope of dishes, including those that generally required elaborate cooking techniques. Sous-vide cooking, acceptance warming, and vacuum-fixing procedures turned out to be important for the culinary munitions stockpile, improving the quality and assortment of menu contributions.

The development of menu decisions additionally answered the rising interest for customization. Railroad cooking administrations embraced advanced stages that permitted travelers to pre-request feasts, determine dietary inclinations, and even modify their dishes. This degree of personalization upgraded the general eating experience as well as mirrored a shift towards client driven approaches in railroad providing food.

An unmistakable part of the developing menu decisions is the recharged accentuation on provincial and neighborhood flavors. Current railroad menus commend the culinary legacy of the areas crossed by the trains. Nearby strengths, obtained from provincial makers and providers, add a bona fide touch to the eating experience. Whether it's exhibiting the kinds of a particular Indian state or featuring the culinary practices of an European district, railroad menus have turned into a material for celebrating neighborhood gastronomy.

As of late, manageability has arisen as a significant thought in menu decisions. Railroad cooking administrations progressively focus on eco-accommodating works on, including obtaining neighborhood and occasional fixings, limiting food squander, and embracing earth cognizant bundling. Travelers are presently bound to find menu choices that line up with their upsides of manageability and moral feasting.

The joining of innovation and information investigation has additionally refined menu decisions on trains. Railroad organizations influence traveler criticism, dietary inclinations, and utilization examples to upgrade their menus persistently. This information driven approach guarantees that the menu decisions reverberate with the inclinations of the travelers, making a more customized and charming feasting experience.

The current scene of rail route menu decisions mirrors a different embroidery of flavors, taking special care of a wide range of tastes and inclinations. Connoisseur choices coincide with solace food works of art, and the coordination of worldwide impacts has enhanced the culinary contributions on trains. The developing menus are a demonstration of the unique idea of rail route providing food, where advancement, culinary craftsmanship, and a profound comprehension of traveler assumptions merge.

3.3 Passenger favorites and their cultural significance

Traveler top picks on railroad menus are something other than culinary decisions; they are emblematic portrayals of social inclinations, provincial personalities, and the common encounters of those setting out on a train venture. These cherished dishes act as social ministers, spanning holes between different foundations and making a feeling of association among travelers who meet up on the shared conviction of shared dinners.

With regards to Indian railroad cooking, the omnipresent Chicken Curry stands apart as a traveler #1 with significant social importance. This dish, with its sweet-smelling mix of flavors and delicious chicken, mirrors the rich culinary customs of India. Every area in India has its own special interpretation of Chicken Curry, consolidating nearby flavors, cooking procedures, and flavor profiles. As a traveler #1, Chicken Curry turns into an image of the different and energetic embroidery of Indian cooking, welcoming explorers to leave on a gastronomic excursion through the country's culinary scene.

Biryani, another Indian rail route menu number one, holds an exceptional spot in the hearts of travelers. This fragrant and delightful rice dish, frequently including meat or vegetables, is a culinary wonder that grandstands the complicated layering of flavors and the creativity of slow-cooking. Biryani isn't only a dish; a social symbol conveys verifiable importance, addressing the combination of Mughlai and native Indian culinary practices. Its presence on railroad menus offers travelers a sample of the magnificence and intricacy that characterizes Indian food.

Getting across landmasses, the adored American work of art, the Cheeseburger, has turned into a notable traveler number one with social reverberation. This humble yet generally revered dish, highlighting a ground meat patty settled in a bun, epitomizes the soul of American cheap food culture. The Burger's prominence on rail line menus reflects an inclination for its natural taste as well as the worldwide impact of American culinary practices. It fills in as a social extension, rising above boundaries and carrying a cut of History of the U.S to travelers from different foundations.

In the domain of European rail route travel, the exemplary Croissant holds a unique spot as a traveler number one with social importance. Beginning from France, the rich and flaky layers of the Croissant have become inseparable from the class and refinement of French baked good. Its consideration on railroad menus, whether served plain or as a component of a morning meal gathering, brings out the appeal of French bistros and adds a bit of mainland refinement to the movement experience.

The getting through prominence of Pasta dishes, for example, Spaghetti Bolognese and Pasta Pomodoro, on rail route menus mirrors the social impact of Italian cook-ing. The guileful mix of pasta with rich, exquisite sauces and sweet-smelling spices addresses the general allure of Italian flavors. These dishes have become top choices among travelers, rising above social limits and offering a sample of the Mediterranean on train ventures.

In Asian railroad travel, the social meaning of dishes like Ramen or Sushi stretches out past their culinary allure. Ramen, with its encouraging noodles and tasty stock, exemplifies the spirit warming quintessence of Japanese food. Its prominence on rail-road menus acquaints travelers with the imaginativeness and effortlessness that char-acterize Japanese culinary customs. Also, Sushi, with its careful readiness and show, addresses the accuracy and equilibrium innate in Japanese gastronomy. These dishes become social diplomats, welcoming travelers to encounter the subtleties of Asian culinary legacy.

The English work of art, Fried fish and French fries, holds an esteemed put on railroad menus, especially with regards to prepare travel in the Unified Realm. This quintessential dish, including battered and seared fish with a side of fresh fries, isn't simply a dinner; it is a social establishment. Fried fish and French fries inspire the wistfulness of ocean side towns and customary English bars, offering travelers a sample of culinary legacy and an association with the social texture of the locale.

In South America, the social meaning of Empanadas as a traveler most loved is significant. These exquisite turnovers, loaded up with meat, cheddar, or vegetables, are not only a bite; they are significant of the different culinary customs that length the mainland. Whether getting a charge out of Argentinian-style empanadas with delightful meat fillings or Chilean varieties with fish, travelers are blessed to receive a culinary excursion through the rich embroidery of South American flavors.

With regards to Center Eastern rail line travel, the social meaning of dishes like Shawarma or Falafel as traveler top picks is well established. Shawarma, with its delicious layers of flavored meat, and Falafel, produced using ground chickpeas or fava beans, are culinary representatives of Center Eastern road food culture. These dishes, with their striking flavors and sweet-smelling flavors, transport travelers to clamoring markets and energetic food scenes, offering a sample of the social lavishness that characterizes the locale.

As travelers set out on their excursions, the most loved dishes on rail line menus become something beyond feasts; they become necessary parts of the movement experience. The social meaning of these dishes lies in their flavors as well as in their capacity to bring out recollections, fashion associations, and act as channels for divided encounters between different voyagers.

Traveler top choices frequently mirror a sensitive harmony among commonality and a feeling of experience. Whether it's appreciating the soothing notes of Chicken Curry on an Indian train, savoring the effortlessness of a Croissant in an European eating vehicle, or partaking in the worldwide allure of a Burger on an American railroad, these dishes become strings that wind around together the social mosaic of train travel.

Chapter 4

The Logistics of Flavor

The coordinated factors of flavor with regards to rail route providing food address an intricate transaction of culinary creativity, store network the board, and the exceptional difficulties presented by the powerful climate of train travel. In the background, a carefully coordinated process unfurls to guarantee that the different and delightful flavors presented on rail line menus arrive at travelers with accuracy and greatness.

At the core of the operations of flavor lies the obtaining of fixings, an interaction that includes a sensitive dance between nearby realness and worldwide impacts. Rail route cooking administrations endeavor to integrate provincial and occasional produce into their menus, mirroring the culinary personality of the areas navigated by the trains. This obligation to realness stretches out to obtaining flavors, meats, vegetables, and other key fixings from nearby providers, guaranteeing a certified portrayal of flavors.

The planned operations of flavor likewise require a profound comprehension of the extraordinary difficulties presented via train travel. The cadenced movement, differing temperatures, and restricted extra room require cautious thought in the choice and planning of fixings.

Transient things should be taken care of with accuracy to keep up with newness, and the bundling should endure the afflictions of movement. Gourmet specialists and kitchen staff are culinary specialists as well as capable issue solvers, exploring the coordinated operations of flavor in a dynamic and steadily evolving climate.

Shipping new and tasty fixings to the installed kitchens is a strategic riddle that rail line catering administrations consistently refine. The combination of present day innovations, like refrigerated stockpiling and transportation, guarantees that the honesty of short-lived things is safeguarded all through the excursion. This obligation to newness isn't just a culinary thought yet additionally a strategic basic to meet traveler assumptions for excellent dinners.

In the domain of railroad cooking, menu arranging is a basic strategic step that includes a nuanced comprehension of traveler inclinations, dietary limitations, and social variety. The operations of flavor reach out past the simple determination of dishes; they include the curation of menus that offer a reasonable and various scope of culinary encounters. Rail route menus become a painstakingly created orchestra of flavors, with each dish assuming an unmistakable part in the gastronomic excursion of the travelers.

The operations of flavor likewise converge with the globalized idea of train travel. As trains cross worldwide lines, the test of keeping up with validness while obliging different palates turns out to be more articulated. Rail route catering administrations should explore the subtleties of territorial foods, adjust to social inclinations, and deal an amicable mix of flavors that resounds with travelers from various regions of the planet. This strategic intricacy requires a fine harmony between normalized contributions and locale explicit claims to fame.

The locally available kitchens of trains act as the focal point of the operations of flavor. In this restricted space, gourmet specialists and kitchen staff work with accuracy and proficiency to change crude fixings into culinary joys. The reception of present day cooking procedures, for example, sous-vide cooking and enlistment warming, adds a layer of refinement to the operations of flavor, considering the readiness of dishes that satisfy high culinary guidelines even in the difficult states of a moving train.

The planning of food readiness is a basic calculated thought. Dinners should be arranged flawlessly to line up with the timetables of the train venture. The test of serving hot, tasty dishes to travelers at assigned feast times requires fastidious preparation and coordination. Gourmet experts become amazing at timing, guaranteeing that each dish is plated and given a similar degree of greatness no matter what the difficulties presented by the train's development.

The planned operations of flavor reach out to the introduction of dishes, changing every feast into a visual and tangible experience. Imaginative plating procedures, creative embellishments, and tender loving care hoist the eating experience on trains. The style of the show are not simply a culinary thrive but rather a calculated thought that adds to the general fulfillment of travelers, transforming every dinner into a snapshot of enjoyment.

The combination of innovation has altered the planned operations of flavor in rail line catering. On the web and portable based food requesting frameworks permit travelers to get to menus, modify their inclinations, and pre-request feasts. This mechanical development upgrades traveler comfort as well as smoothes out the coordinated factors of planning dinners ahead of time, guaranteeing a consistent and productive feasting experience on trains.

In the strategies of flavor, versatility is a key trait. Rail line catering administrations should be light-footed and receptive to the consistently changing requests of travelers, occasional varieties, and unanticipated difficulties. The capacity to make do, improve, and investigate turns into a significant range of abilities as culinary experts and kitchen staff explore the coordinated operations of flavor in the unique setting of train travel.

Squander the board is a fundamental piece of the strategies of flavor, underscoring maintainability and dependable practices. Kitchen staff go through preparing on upgrading fixing use, decreasing abundance bundling, and carrying out eco-accommodating practices. This obligation to limiting waste lines up with more extensive worldwide worries about natural effect and adds to a more feasible way to deal with rail line cooking.

Strategies likewise assume a critical part in the conveyance of dinners inside the train. The productive coordination of serving staff, the synchronization of feast conveyance with the train plan, and the administration of eating spaces all add to the consistent execution of the operations of flavor. Travelers anticipate delectable feasts as well as an efficient and charming eating experience.

4.1 Logistic challenges in transporting and serving food on moving trains

The coordinated operations of shipping and serving food on moving trains present a one of a kind arrangement of difficulties that require creative arrangements, fastidious preparation, and a profound comprehension of the powerful climate of rail travel. From obtaining fixings to coordinating the exact timing of feast administration, rail route providing food administrations explore a perplexing scene to guarantee that travelers experience a consistent and pleasant culinary excursion.

One of the essential difficulties in the coordinated operations of shipping and serving food on moving trains lies in the protection of newness. The cadenced movement, vibrations, and shifting temperatures experienced during train travel can influence the nature of transitory fixings. To address this test, rail route catering administrations put resources into best in class refrigeration and capacity frameworks. These frameworks are intended to keep up with the ideal circumstances for protecting the newness of fixings all through the excursion.

Obtaining new and great fixings is a strategic riddle that rail line cooking administrations constantly refine. The test lies in distinguishing legitimate providers as well as in laying out a smoothed out store network that guarantees a consistent and solid progression of fixings to the locally available kitchens. Nearby obtaining turns into a need to catch the realness of provincial flavors, and organizations with believed providers assume a significant part in beating calculated obstacles.

The restricted extra room locally available trains represents one more critical test in the strategies of shipping and serving food. Kitchens on trains are much of the time smaller, and the capacity limit is streamlined for productivity. Cooks and kitchen staff should cautiously plan fixing position, taking into account factors, for example, openness, temperature zones, and the requirement for speedy recovery during dinner readiness. This strategic riddle requires a fastidious comprehension of the installed kitchen design and the spatial imperatives inborn in a moving train.

Keeping up with the sensitive equilibrium of flavors during travel is a culinary and strategic test. Flavors, sauces, and preparing profiles should be painstakingly aligned to endure the varieties in temperature and the requirements of extra room. The coordinated operations of flavor conservation become a necessary piece of recipe improvement, with culinary experts utilizing methods that upgrade the power of flavors, guaranteeing that each dish arrives at travelers with its expected taste profile.

The planning of dinner administration is a basic calculated thought. Travelers expect hot and newly pre-arranged dinners served at assigned feast times, no matter what the difficulties presented by the train's development. Gourmet specialists and kitchen staff should synchronize the readiness of dishes with the train plan, considering variables like stops, speed varieties, and the span of the excursion. This exact coordination requires a profound comprehension of the calculated complexities of train travel.

In the coordinated operations of shipping and serving food on moving trains, bundling turns into a vital component. Feasts should be bundled in a manner that guarantees they stay in one piece and outwardly engaging regardless of the movement of the train. The bundling must likewise add to temperature maintenance, safeguarding the newness and warmth of the food until it arrives at the traveler's table. Rail route cooking administrations put resources into bundling arrangements that work out some kind of harmony between usefulness, feel, and supportability.

The coordination of serving staff adds one more layer of intricacy to the operations of dinner administration on trains. Serving staff should explore the moving train, conveying dinners with accuracy and mindfulness. The strategic test lies in preparing staff to expect and adjust to the exceptional states of the eating vehicle, guaranteeing that travelers get an elevated degree of administration in spite of the unique climate.

Traveler inclinations and dietary limitations further confound the coordinated factors of dinner administration. Rail route providing food administrations should be prepared to deal with a different scope of dietary necessities, including veggie lover, vegetarian, sans gluten, and other explicit solicitations. The strategies of customization require smoothed out correspondence between travelers, providing food administrations, and locally available staff to guarantee that singular necessities are met without compromising the proficiency of the general help.

The coordinated operations of shipping and serving food on moving trains cross with the worldwide idea of rail travel. Trains crossing worldwide lines should explore the complexities of customs guidelines, sanitation norms, and provincial culinary inclinations. Rail route providing food administrations should adjust their coordinated operations to line up with the social subtleties of every district, guaranteeing that the dinners served resound with the assorted foundations of travelers.

Squander the executives is an essential piece of the coordinated factors of railroad providing food, stressing manageability and mindful practices. On moving trains, the test lies in limiting waste age while effectively taking care of and discarding leftover materials. Rail line cooking administrations execute squander decrease procedures, for example, advancing fixing utilization, taking on eco-accommodating bundling, and empowering travelers to partake in manageable practices.

The combination of innovation has turned into a distinct advantage in the strategies of railroad cooking. On the web and versatile based food requesting frameworks permit travelers to get to menus, modify their inclinations, and pre-request feasts. This mechanical development improves traveler comfort as well as smoothes out the strategies of planning dinners ahead of time, guaranteeing a consistent and effective feasting experience on trains.

Constant information examination and correspondence advances assume a pivotal part in the operations of shipping and serving food on moving trains. Rail route providing food administrations influence information to follow traveler inclinations, screen stock levels, and smooth out the production network.

This information driven approach improves the deftness and responsiveness of providing food administrations, permitting them to adjust to changing conditions and advance the effectiveness of feast administration.

4.2 Preservation methods to maintain taste and quality

Safeguarding the taste and nature of food on moving trains represents an unmistakable arrangement of difficulties, requiring imaginative protection strategies that take special care of the powerful climate of rail travel. From the obtaining of fixings to the last show of feasts, rail line catering administrations utilize a scope of safeguarding strategies to guarantee that travelers experience similar degree of culinary greatness regardless of the difficulties presented by the excursion.

The conservation of newness starts with the cautious obtaining of fixings. Railroad providing food administrations focus on neighborhood and occasional produce to catch the valid kinds of the areas crossed by the trains. The accentuation on neighborhood obtaining not just adds a local touch to the dinners yet in addition lessens the strategic difficulties related with significant distance transportation. By choosing the freshest fixings from solid providers, rail line cooking administrations establish the groundwork for keeping up with taste and quality.

Refrigeration and cold stockpiling assume a urgent part in protecting the newness of short-lived fixings during travel. Locally available kitchens are furnished with best in class refrigeration frameworks that keep up with ideal temperatures for different food things. The test lies in adjusting these frameworks to the powerful states of a moving train, where vibrations and temperature varieties are intrinsic. Effective refrigeration forestalls waste as well as guarantees that fixings hold their surface, flavor, and dietary benefit.

Vacuum fixing is a safeguarding technique that has found far and wide application in rail line cooking. This procedure includes eliminating air from bundling to make a vacuum, forestalling the oxidation and decay of food. Vacuum-fixed fixings, for example, marinated meats or pre-cooked dishes, experience broadened time span of usability without settling on taste. This technique is especially compelling in saving the respectability of flavors during the excursion, as it limits openness to outer components.

Freezing is one more fundamental conservation strategy utilized in rail route taking special care of expand the life span of fixings. Fast freezing procedures assist with keeping up with the surface and taste of food sources while forestalling the arrangement of ice precious stones that can influence quality. Frozen fixings, from vegetables to pre-arranged feasts, offer a helpful and productive method for guaranteeing a steady stockpile of crisp tasting things during the whole excursion.

Drying out is a conservation technique that lessens the dampness content of food varieties, hindering the development of microscopic organisms and microorganisms. While customarily connected with dried natural products or tidbits, present day drying out procedures are utilized in rail line taking special care of protect a large number of fixings. Dried out spices, flavors, and, surprisingly, certain sauces can be rehydrated during the cooking system, permitting culinary specialists to inject dishes with concentrated flavors.

Canning is a dependable conservation technique that assumes a vital part in keeping up with the taste and nature of food sources on moving trains. Fixings are fixed in impermeable compartments and intensity handled to obliterate microbes, forestalling decay. Canned products, like sauces, stews, or cured things, are strong to the difficulties of train travel and hold their flavors overstretched periods. This conservation technique guarantees a steady inventory of fixings that add to the general taste profile of dinners.

Changed climate bundling (Guide) is a protection procedure that includes changing the piece of gases inside food bundling to dial back the weakening system. By controlling the degrees of oxygen, carbon dioxide, and nitrogen, Guide broadens the time span of usability of transitory things. This strategy is especially compelling for saving pre-bundled feasts, mixed greens, and other new things on moving trains, keeping up with both taste and visual allure.

In the domain of bread shop and cake things, controlled climate capacity is a safeguarding strategy that guarantees the newness of bread, baked goods, and treats. By managing temperature, stickiness, and gas sythesis inside capacity units, this strategy forestalls the untimely staling of prepared merchandise. The test lies in adjusting these controlled airs to the restricted spaces of locally available storage spaces, where space advancement is fundamental.

Airtight fixed bundling is a safeguarding technique that makes a water/air proof and impermeable seal around food things, shielding them from outside pollutants. This method is usually applied to individual servings of fixings, sauces, or pre-bundled feasts. The airtight seal goes about as a hindrance against the entrance of air, dampness, and scents, guaranteeing that the flavors are safeguarded until the second the traveler opens the bundle.

Protecting the taste and nature of refreshments on moving trains includes special difficulties, especially in keeping up with the temperature and flavor profiles of hot and cold beverages. Protected compartments and warm carafes assume an essential part in keeping drinks at the ideal temperatures during administration. The coordinated operations of refreshment safeguarding likewise reach out to the cautious treatment of sensitive things like wine or champagne, where temperature control and capacity conditions are vital to keeping up with taste and quality.

The coordination of present day cooking strategies into installed kitchens adds to the conservation of flavors. Sous-vide cooking, for instance, includes vacuum-fixing fixings and slow-cooking them at exact temperatures. This strategy improves the delicacy and flavor maintenance of meats, guaranteeing that travelers experience an elevated degree of culinary greatness notwithstanding the difficulties of train travel. Acceptance warming is another innovation that takes into consideration exact control of cooking temperatures, adding to the general protection of flavors.

The conservation of taste and quality likewise reaches out to the last phases of feast readiness, where inventive plating and show methods add to the general eating experience. Culinary experts on moving trains use embellishments, sauces, and imaginative plating to improve the visual allure of dishes. This fastidious meticulousness hoists the tasteful part of dinners as well as adds to the safeguarding of the tactile components that make each dish noteworthy.

4.3 Technology and infrastructure improvements in food transportation

Headways in innovation and framework have changed the scene of food transportation with regards to rail line catering. From obtaining fixings to the last conveyance of feasts, these developments have essentially improved proficiency, quality, and the general eating experience for travelers on moving trains. The collaboration of innovation and framework upgrades assumes a urgent part in conquering the strategic difficulties related with moving food in the powerful climate of rail travel.

One of the critical mechanical progressions in food transportation is the execution of continuous following and checking frameworks. RFID (Radio-Recurrence Distinguishing proof) and GPS (Worldwide Situating Framework) advances are coordinated into the strategies chain, permitting rail route catering administrations to follow the development and area of food shipments definitively. This degree of perceivability empowers proactive navigation, guaranteeing that fixings and feasts arrive at their objections on time and in ideal condition.

The coordination of cloud-based stock administration frameworks has smoothed out the obtaining and stockpiling of fixings in railroad providing food. These frameworks give a unified stage to overseeing obtainment, stock levels, and provider connections. Cloud-based arrangements offer ongoing updates, working with consistent correspondence between providers, kitchen staff, and the board. The openness and straightforwardness given by these frameworks add to effective production network the executives and further developed dynamic in obtaining great fixings.

Present day refrigeration and capacity innovations play had a critical impact in safeguarding the newness of fixings during travel. High level refrigeration units on trains are outfitted with temperature control includes that adjust to the powerful states of rail travel. The joining of superior execution protection materials guarantees that transient things stay at ideal temperatures, alleviating the effect of vibrations and temperature minor departure from the moving train. These innovations add to keeping up with the taste and nature of fixings all through the excursion.

The reception of cutting edge kitchen gear has changed installed kitchens into culinary center points prepared to fulfill the needs of connoisseur feasting on trains. Enlistment burners, combi stoves, and sous-vide machines have become standard apparatuses in present day rail route kitchens. These machines offer exact temperature control, productive cooking times, and the adaptability to execute a different scope of culinary methods. The reconciliation of such high level gear adds to the safeguarding of flavors and the arrangement of top notch dinners in the bound spaces of moving trains.

In the domain of food bundling, innovation plays had an essential impact in guaranteeing the safeguarding of taste and quality. Vacuum-fixing machines, for example, are utilized to eliminate air from bundling, making a vacuum seal that limits openness to outer components. This conservation technique expands the timeframe of realistic usability of pre-arranged dishes, marinated meats, and different fixings. The utilization of eco-accommodating and reasonable bundling materials is likewise a region where innovative progressions line up with natural contemplations, offering both safeguarding benefits and a guarantee to mindful practices.

On the web and versatile based food requesting frameworks address a huge mechanical jump in improving traveler comfort and smoothing out the strategies of food transportation. Travelers can get to computerized menus, alter their inclinations, and pre-request dinners before their excursion. This advancement speeds up the food planning process as well as takes into account better coordination between the kitchen staff and serving group, guaranteeing that feasts are conveyed to travelers productively during assigned dinner times.

The use of information examination in railroad cooking has turned into a unique advantage in enhancing food transportation coordinated factors. By utilizing traveler information, utilization examples, and input, providing food administrations can fit their menus and stock administration techniques to meet the inclinations of their customer base. Prescient investigation likewise empower proactive direction, helping railroad providing food administrations expect request vacillations, streamline fixing acquirement, and upgrade by and large functional productivity.

The mix of temperature-controlled holders in food transportation has tended to one of the basic difficulties in saving taste and quality. These specific compartments give a controlled climate that manages temperature, moistness, and ventilation, protecting the newness of fixings and feasts during travel. The holders are intended to endure the vibrations and development related with train travel, offering a dependable answer for moving short-lived things without settling for less on quality.

Versatile kitchens, furnished with cutting edge cooking offices, have arisen as a progressive framework improvement in rail line providing food. These measured kitchens are decisively situated at key areas, considering the effective arrangement of feasts near takeoff focuses. Versatile kitchens improve adaptability in providing food tasks, empowering cooks to adjust to territorial inclinations, occasional accessibility of fixings, and explicit dietary prerequisites. This foundation improvement adds to the general protection of taste and quality by working with the in a hurry planning of new and modified dinners.

High velocity trains and present day rail framework play likewise had an impact in upgrading food transportation operations. The decrease in movement time related with high velocity trains limits the term that dinners are on the way, adding to the safeguarding of taste and newness. Updated rail networks with smoother tracks and diminished vibrations further help the transportation of fragile food things, guaranteeing that fixings and arranged dishes arrive at their objective with insignificant effect on quality.

The execution of brought together kitchens, decisively situated along rail courses, is a foundation improvement that upgrades the proficiency of food transportation. These brought together offices act as centers for fixing planning, cooking, and bundling. By solidifying these cycles in a concentrated area, railroad providing food administrations can enhance the utilization of assets, smooth out operations, and guarantee predictable quality across various train ventures.

The coming of savvy bundling advancements has presented developments that go past conventional protection strategies. Shrewd bundling consolidates highlights like temperature sensors, newness markers, and intelligent names that give ongoing data about the state of the items. These innovations empower the two travelers and catering administrations to screen the newness of dinners, adding to a more straightforward and informed food transportation process.

Mechanization and advanced mechanics have tracked down application in different parts of food transportation operations, especially in the readiness and bundling stages. Mechanized frameworks for fixing parceling, cleaving, and blending improve accuracy and effectiveness in kitchen activities. Mechanical technology in bundling smooth out the fixing and naming cycles, adding to the protection of taste and quality by limiting the gamble of human blunder.

Chapter 5

Tales from the Pantry Car

Stories from the storage room vehicle reveal an intriguing story of culinary craftsmanship, calculated dominance, and the novel difficulties looked by the uncelebrated yet truly great individuals of railroad cooking. Settled inside the moving bounds of a train, the storeroom vehicle is a culinary center where cooks and kitchen staff organize a gastronomic orchestra, changing crude fixings into scrumptious feasts that navigate different scenes and societies. In the background, these culinary maestros explore a powerful climate, winding around stories through the flavors, fragrances, and shared encounters of train travel.

The storeroom vehicle isn't simply a kitchen on wheels; it is a microcosm of inventiveness and productivity, where cooks use their culinary ability to defeat the difficulties presented via train travel. As the train tears across tracks, the storage room vehicle turns into a culinary material where gourmet specialists paint with flavors, injecting dishes with local flavors that charm the palates of travelers from different foundations. This portable kitchen is a demonstration of flexibility and development, where each excursion delivers another arrangement of culinary undertakings.

The excursion starts with fastidious preparation in the storage room vehicle, where cooks curate menus that mirror the variety of the locales navigated. The test lies in creating menus that take care of the inclinations of an expansive range of travelers while guaranteeing the plausibility of readiness inside the restricted space of the moving train. The storage room vehicle is a center point of menu designing, where gourmet experts balance the commonality of exemplary dishes with the energy of local fortes, making a culinary excursion that reflects the train's actual direction.

The obtaining of elements for the storage room vehicle is a calculated riddle that unfurls across stations and boundaries. Gourmet specialists should expect the accessibility of new, great produce at different stops along the course. Neighborhood markets become the storage space vehicle's gold mine, offering a variety of flavors, vegetables, and meats that become the structure blocks of culinary greatness. The test isn't simply in getting fixings yet in addition in adjusting to the irregularity and provincial subtleties that characterize the culinary scene.

In the storage room vehicle, gourmet experts become narrators, mixing each dish with social importance and authentic setting. A straightforward curry turns into a story of zest shipping lanes, a biryani reverberations stories of Mughal glory, and an unassuming sandwich mirrors the worldwide impacts forming present day food. The storage room vehicle is a phase where culinary stories unfurl, welcoming travelers to participate in a tactile excursion that rises above the actual limits of the train.

The cadenced movement of the train presents a special test in the storage room vehicle, where cooks should offset accuracy with versatility. From slashing vegetables to stewing sauces, each culinary move should synchronize with the rhythm of the moving train. The storeroom vehicle's kitchen staff become amazing at timing, guaranteeing that each dish is plated and given a similar degree of greatness, no matter what the difficulties presented by the train's development.

As the storage space vehicle navigates scenes, it turns into a portable study hall where cooks bestow their culinary insight to kitchen staff. The kinship inside the storeroom vehicle is a demonstration of the common enthusiasm for food and the aggregate obligation to conveying an outstanding eating experience. Junior culinary specialists gain proficiency with the craft of flavor adjusting, the complexities of local flavors, and the spontaneous creation expected to adjust to the steadily changing storeroom of fixings on a moving train.

The storage room vehicle isn't safe to the unforeseen, and culinary experts should be prepared to ad lib when confronted with difficulties like deferrals, redirections, or changes in the accessibility of fixings. Adaptability turns into a culinary righteousness, and cooks in the storage room vehicle embrace the unusualness of train travel, transforming impediments into open doors for culinary development. It is inside this powerful climate that the genuine creativity of the storeroom vehicle unfurls.

In the storage room vehicle, culinary specialists are not simply cooks; they are calculated planners who plan proficient work processes to streamline the utilization of room and assets. The bound kitchen space requests imagination in gear design, fixing capacity, and cooking procedures. Every last trace of the storage room vehicle is used in a calculated manner, changing it into a versatile culinary studio where cooks arrange a consistent dance of flavors.

The storage space vehicle is a demonstration of the worldwide impact on culinary customs, where cooks curate menus that rise above borders and carry the world to the eating tables of travelers. The diverse blend of dishes reflects the social mosaic of train travel, offering travelers a sample of various districts without leaving their seats. In the storage room vehicle, the culinary excursion isn't simply an actual one; a social odyssey unfurls plate by plate.

The storeroom vehicle is a domain of tangible enjoyment, where the smell of flavors, the sizzle of fixings, and the orchestra of flavors merge to make a multisensory experience for travelers. Culinary specialists in the storeroom vehicle grasp the significant effect of fragrances on taste discernment, and they utilize this information to improve the general feasting experience. The floating fragrances from the storage room vehicle become a preface to the culinary stories that anticipate travelers in the eating vehicles.

Dinner administration in the storage room vehicle is a very much arranged presentation, where gourmet specialists and serving staff team up to convey a culinary display. The test lies in synchronizing the planning of feast arrangement with the train plan, guaranteeing that hot, delightful dishes arrive at travelers at assigned dinner times. The storeroom vehicle turns into a center point of movement as cooks plate dishes with accuracy, realizing that every feast is a culinary diplomat addressing the kinds of the excursion.

The storage room vehicle stretches out past conventional dinner administration, embracing the pattern of culinary customization. Travelers, outfitted with computerized menus, practice their inclinations and dietary decisions, customizing their culinary excursion. The storeroom vehicle's kitchen staff capably handle these modified solicitations, adding a layer of individualization to the feasting experience. It is inside the limits of the storage room vehicle that the culinary group changes traveler inclinations into tailor-made gastronomic manifestations.

The storeroom vehicle isn't resistant to the call of advancement, and culinary specialists influence present day cooking strategies to raise the locally available eating experience. Sous-vide cooking, enlistment warming, and sub-atomic gastronomy find their direction into the storeroom vehicle's culinary collection, adding a contemporary turn to customary top picks. These advancements not just grandstand the culinary ability of the gourmet specialists yet additionally add to the safeguarding of taste and quality in the unique climate of the moving train.

The storeroom vehicle fills in as an extension between culinary legacy and contemporary patterns, offering a mix of immortal works of art and present day gastronomic joys. Gourmet specialists take motivation from local culinary practices, implanting their manifestations with legitimacy, while likewise embracing the advancing sense of taste of the present travelers. The storage space vehicle turns into a culinary time container, safeguarding the quintessence of customary dishes while embracing the soul of culinary development.

In the storage space vehicle, gourmet specialists are not only suppliers of food; they are custodians of recollections. The feasting experience on a moving train rises above the demonstration of eating; it turns into a noteworthy part in the movement story of travelers. Culinary specialists in the storeroom vehicle grasp the profound reverberation of food and endeavor to make dishes that bring out a feeling of spot, an association with social legacy, and a common kinship among travelers.

The storage room vehicle is a material of manageability, where cooks and kitchen staff effectively participate in squander decrease rehearses. From upgrading fixing use to taking on eco-accommodating bundling, the storage room vehicle embraces a pledge to mindful culinary practices. The excursion towards manageability isn't simply a culinary pattern however a cognizant work to limit the ecological impression of installed eating.

5.1 Stories of the pantry car, a mobile kitchen on trains

The storage space vehicle, a portable kitchen on trains, arises as a story embroidery woven with accounts of culinary creativity, strategic artfulness, and the particular difficulties that accompany planning feasts in the powerful climate of moving trains. This culinary safe house on wheels is something other than a space for cooking; it's a domain where gourmet specialists and kitchen staff leave on a gastronomic excursion, changing crude fixings into delightful feasts that cross different scenes and societies. The stories of the storeroom vehicle uncover the substance of rail line providing food, a combination of innovativeness and flexibility against the musical scenery of train travel.

The beginning of each excursion in the storage space vehicle is set apart by fastidious preparation. Cooks curate menus that mirror the variety of the districts the train crosses, a sensitive harmony between meeting the inclinations of a wide range of travelers and the reasonable items of planning dinners inside the restricted space of a moving train. The storage room vehicle, with its steadily evolving menu, is a demonstration of the culinary sharpness expected to make a gastronomic excursion that reflects the train's actual direction.

Obtaining elements for the storage room vehicle is a calculated dance that unfurls across stations and lines. Culinary specialists should expect the accessibility of new, great produce at different stops along the course.

Nearby business sectors become mother lodes, offering a variety of flavors, vegetables, and meats that become the structure blocks of culinary greatness. The test isn't simply in obtaining fixings yet in addition in adjusting to the irregularity and provincial subtleties that characterize the culinary scene.

The storeroom vehicle turns into a phase where cooks make stories through flavors, mixing each dish with social importance and verifiable setting. A basic curry turns into a story of zest shipping lanes, a biryani reverberations stories of Mughal greatness, and an unassuming sandwich mirrors the worldwide impacts forming current cooking. The storage room vehicle is a space where culinary narrating isn't bound to words yet unfurls through the fragrances and flavors that enamor the feelings of travelers.

The cadenced movement of the train adds a layer of intricacy to the stories of the storeroom vehicle. Cooks should offset accuracy with versatility as they explore the difficulties presented by vibrations and development. Each culinary move, from hacking vegetables to stewing sauces, should synchronize with the rhythm of the moving train. The storeroom vehicle's kitchen staff become amazing at timing, guaranteeing that each dish is plated and given a similar degree of greatness, no matter what the difficulties presented by the train's development.

The storage space vehicle turns into a portable homeroom where gourmet experts give their culinary insight to kitchen staff. The kinship inside the storage space vehicle is a demonstration of the common energy for food and the aggregate obligation to conveying an outstanding feasting experience. Junior cooks gain proficiency with the craft of flavor adjusting, the complexities of local flavors, and the impromptu creation expected to adjust to the consistently changing storeroom of fixings on a moving train. The stories of the storage space vehicle reach out past culinary craftsmanship; they epitomize a custom of mentorship and expertise move that guarantees the progression of greatness.

Adaptability turns into a culinary temperance in the storeroom vehicle, as cooks should be prepared to ad lib when confronted with difficulties like postponements, redirections, or changes in the accessibility of fixings. The bound space requests imagination in hardware design, fixing capacity, and cooking strategies. The storage space vehicle isn't simply a kitchen; it's a unique work area where cooks organize a consistent dance of flavors, adjusting to the surprising and transforming deterrents into potential open doors for culinary development.

In the storeroom vehicle, culinary specialists are not simply cooks; they are strategic modelers who plan effective work processes to upgrade the utilization of room and assets. Every last bit of the storage space vehicle is used in a calculated way, changing it into a versatile culinary studio where gourmet experts arrange a consistent dance of flavors. The stories of the storeroom vehicle highlight the cooperative energy of culinary creativity and calculated accuracy expected to convey connoisseur dinners in the bound space of a moving train.

The storeroom vehicle is an extension between culinary legacy and contemporary patterns, offering a mix of immortal works of art and present day gastronomic pleasures. Cooks take motivation from territorial culinary practices, implanting their manifestations with credibility, while additionally embracing the developing sense of taste of the present travelers. The storage space vehicle turns into a culinary time container, protecting the pith of customary dishes while embracing the soul of culinary development. The stories of the storeroom vehicle mirror the gourmet specialists' obligation to respecting culinary practices while persistently pushing the limits of development.

The storeroom vehicle fills in as a tactile enjoyment, where the fragrance of flavors, the sizzle of fixings, and the orchestra of flavors unite to make a multisensory experience for travelers. Gourmet specialists in the storeroom vehicle figure out the significant effect of smells on taste discernment, and they utilize this information to upgrade the general eating experience. The floating fragrances from the storeroom vehicle become a preface to the culinary stories that anticipate travelers in the eating vehicles.

Feast administration in the storage room vehicle is a very much arranged exhibition, where gourmet experts and serving staff team up to convey a culinary display. The test lies in synchronizing the planning of dinner arrangement with the train plan, guaranteeing that hot, delightful dishes arrive at travelers at assigned feast times. The storeroom vehicle turns into a center of movement as gourmet experts plate dishes with accuracy, realizing that every feast is a culinary minister addressing the kinds of the excursion.

The storage space vehicle stretches out past customary feast administration, embracing the pattern of culinary customization. Travelers, outfitted with computerized menus, practice their inclinations and dietary decisions, customizing their culinary excursion. The storage room vehicle's kitchen staff skillfully handle these modified solicitations, adding a layer of individualization to the eating experience. It is inside the limits of the storage room vehicle that the culinary group changes traveler inclinations into tailor-made gastronomic manifestations.

The storage space vehicle isn't invulnerable to the call of development, and culinary experts influence present day cooking strategies to raise the locally available feasting experience. Sous-vide cooking, enlistment warming, and sub-atomic gastronomy find their direction into the storeroom vehicle's culinary collection, adding a contemporary bend to customary top choices. These advancements not just feature the culinary ability of the gourmet experts yet in addition add to the conservation of taste and quality in the unique climate of the moving train.

In the storage space vehicle, gourmet experts are not only suppliers of food; they are custodians of recollections. The feasting experience on a moving train rises above the demonstration of eating; it turns into a noteworthy section in the movement story of travelers. Culinary experts in the storeroom vehicle grasp the close to home reverberation of food and endeavor to make dishes that summon a feeling of spot, an association with social legacy, and a common fellowship among travelers.

The storage space vehicle turns into a material of supportability, where cooks and kitchen staff effectively take part in squander decrease rehearses. From improving fixing use to taking on eco-accommodating bundling, the storeroom vehicle embraces a guarantee to capable culinary practices. The excursion towards maintainability isn't simply a culinary pattern yet a cognizant work to limit the ecological impression of installed eating.

5.2 Experiences of pantry car staff and chefs

The encounters of storeroom vehicle staff and gourmet experts disclose a rich embroidery of difficulties, wins, and the remarkable brotherhood that characterizes life in the powerful climate of a moving train. In the background, in the core of the storage room vehicle, these overlooked yet truly great individuals explore the complexities of rail route providing food, changing each excursion into a culinary exhibition. Their stories reverberate enthusiastically for food, flexibility to consistently evolving conditions, and a common obligation to conveying an outstanding feasting experience for travelers.

Life for storage room vehicle staff and gourmet specialists is an orchestra of development and accuracy. As the train rushes across tracks, the storage space vehicle turns into a domain where gourmet specialists and kitchen staff should synchronize their activities with the musical movement of the train. From hacking vegetables to mixing stewing sauces, each culinary move is a dance that requires both expertise and versatility. The bound space of the storage room vehicle requests a degree of co-ordination that goes past customary kitchens, transforming every feast planning into an agreeable movement of flavors.

The excursion starts with careful preparation as culinary experts curate menus that reflect the topographical direction of the train. The storage room vehicle's kitchen staff should expect the accessibility of new fixings at different stops, frequently drenching themselves in nearby business sectors to source the flavors, vegetables, and meats that will frame the foundation of each dish. The test lies not just in arranging menus that take special care of assorted palates yet additionally in adjusting to the provincial subtleties that impact culinary inclinations along the course.

Adaptability turns into a sign of life in the storeroom vehicle. Deferrals, redirections, and surprising shifts are standard for the direction, requiring cooks and kitchen staff to make do on the fly. Whether confronted with an unexpected flood in travelers or a deficiency of explicit fixings, the capacity to adjust turns into a culinary goodness. These difficulties, as opposed to deterrents, become open doors for development, pushing the culinary limits inside the restricted space of a moving train.

The storage space vehicle isn't simply a work area; it's a portable study hall where the trading of culinary insight happens. Gourmet experts coach junior staff, granting the procedures of cooking as well as the specialty of exploring the exceptional difficulties presented via train travel. The fellowship inside the storage room vehicle is based on a common enthusiasm for food, a guarantee to greatness, and a shared comprehension of the requests of their dynamic climate. These mentorship encounters add to the coherence of culinary practices and the encouraging of another age of cooks.

Each excursion in the storage space vehicle is a tangible encounter, from the sweet-smelling flavors that drift through the air to the sizzle of fixings on hot frying pans. The staff figures out the significant effect of smells on taste discernment and uses this information to improve the general feasting experience. The storage room vehicle turns into a space where the adoration for food isn't simply an expert prerequisite however a common excitement that imbues each dish with energy and commitment.

Feast administration in the storeroom vehicle is a very much planned exhibition, with gourmet experts and serving staff working couple to convey a culinary display. The test lies in synchronizing the planning of dinner readiness with the train plan, guaranteeing that hot, delightful dishes arrive at travelers at assigned feast times. The storage space vehicle turns into a center of action as gourmet experts plate dishes with accuracy, realizing that every dinner is a culinary representative addressing the kinds of the excursion.

Past customary feast administration, the storage space vehicle embraces the pattern of culinary customization. Travelers furnished with advanced menus practice their inclinations and dietary decisions, adding an additional layer of intricacy to the culinary group's liabilities. The staff skillfully handles these modified solicitations, adding a bit of individualization to the feasting experience. It's inside the bounds of the storage space vehicle that the culinary group changes traveler inclinations into tailor-made gastronomic manifestations.

In the storage room vehicle, culinary specialists are not simply cooks; they are guardians of recollections. The feasting experience on a moving train isn't just about food; it turns into an essential part in the movement story of travelers.

Gourmet specialists figure out the close to home reverberation of food and endeavor to make dishes that summon a feeling of spot, an association with social legacy, and a common kinship among travelers. The tales of the storage space vehicle are woven into the texture of these feasting encounters, making minutes that wait in the recollections of the people who set out on the gastronomic excursion.

The storeroom vehicle likewise fills in as a material for manageability rehearses. Cooks and kitchen staff effectively take part in squander decrease, from streamlining fixing use to embracing eco-accommodating bundling. The excursion towards maintainability isn't simply a culinary pattern however a cognizant work to limit the natural impression of installed eating. The staff's obligation to dependable culinary practices reflects their commitment to the art as well as their attention to the more extensive effect of their work.

Amidst the culinary disarray, the storeroom vehicle is a center point of innovativeness and development. Gourmet specialists influence present day cooking methods, from sous-vide cooking to atomic gastronomy, to hoist the locally available eating experience. These developments not just grandstand the culinary ability of the gourmet specialists yet additionally add to the safeguarding of taste and quality in the unique climate of the moving train. The storeroom vehicle turns into a space where custom meets innovation, making a culinary combination that enraptures the palates of travelers.

The encounters of storage room vehicle staff and culinary specialists reach out past the limits of the kitchen. The excursion is set apart by the assorted scenes, societies, and individuals experienced along the course. The storeroom vehicle turns into a portable stage for social trade, where cooks integrate local impacts into their culinary manifestations. The staff's collaborations with travelers give bits of knowledge into the different inclinations and stories that shape the eating experience on a moving train.

Life in the storage space vehicle isn't without its physical and mental requests. The steady development, restricted spaces, and the requirement for versatility require an extraordinary arrangement of abilities and strength. The fellowship among the staff turns into an emotionally supportive network, a common perspective that encourages a feeling of local area inside the storeroom vehicle. These common encounters make a bond that goes past expert obligations, transforming the storeroom vehicle into a versatile family where each part assumes an imperative part in the culinary excursion.

5.3 Memorable moments and challenges faced on the tracks

The tracks of a moving train demonstrate the veracity of a huge number of essential minutes and novel difficulties that characterize the excursion for the two travelers and the devoted group working energetically installed. From stunning scenes that unfurl outside the windows to the complexities of rail route tasks and the powerful climate inside, the tracks become a phase for a horde of encounters that shape the story of train travel.

One of the most captivating parts of train travel is the always changing scene outside the windows. The tracks cut through different scenes, offering travelers an unparalleled view to nature's magnificence. The cadenced clickety-clatter of the wheels turns into a relieving soundtrack to the visual ensemble of mountains, valleys, streams, and fields. These beautiful vistas make enduring impressions, carving themselves into the recollections of travelers who leave on the excursion.

The tracks likewise weave a story of functional complexities, with the train group exploring a trap of operations to guarantee a consistent excursion. From track switches and sign frameworks to organizing plans and overseeing traveler stream, the difficulties looked by the group are all around as differed as the scenes the train navigates. The responsibility and mastery of the rail route staff add to the protected and productive activity of the train, transforming each fruitful excursion into an aggregate accomplishment.

Inside the limits of the train, travelers fashion associations and offer minutes that become the heartbeat of the excursion. The feasting vehicles and parlors become spaces for brotherhood, where outsiders become individual voyagers, trading stories and giggling over shared dinners. The tracks become a conductor for human association, separating hindrances and making a feeling of local area among travelers from different foundations.

Notwithstanding, the tracks likewise present difficulties that require inventiveness and strength. Deferrals, redirections, and surprising stops can disturb the fastidiously arranged venture, testing the persistence of travelers and group the same. Atmospheric conditions, track upkeep, and unexpected occasions add a component of capriciousness to prepare travel. However, it is inside these difficulties that the soul of flexibility and coordinated effort sparkles, as travelers and team meet up to explore the vulnerabilities of the tracks.

The tracks become a material for culinary undertakings, with the storage room vehicle staff and cooks organizing an orchestra of flavors in the midst of the consistent development of the train. Difficulties, for example, keeping up with the newness of fixings, adjusting to the restricted space, and synchronizing feast administration with the train plan add layers of intricacy to the culinary excursion.

The storage room vehicle staff's capacity to change these difficulties into open doors for development guarantees that the tracks become a pathway for gastronomic greatness.

Paramount minutes on the tracks reach out past the visual and culinary domains. They unfurl in the common encounters of travelers, whether it's a fortunate experience with an individual explorer, an unconstrained festival, or the calm impression of a performance venture. The tracks become a phase for individual stories, where people track down comfort, satisfaction, and association inside the cadenced movement of the train.

The difficulties looked on the tracks additionally incorporate the obligation of guaranteeing the prosperity and wellbeing of travelers. Crisis circumstances, clinical episodes, and security concerns request quick and powerful reactions from the team. The tracks become a proving ground for the team's preparation and readiness, featuring the significance of their job in shielding the excursion for everybody locally available.

In the computerized age, the tracks observer the change of train travel into an associated insight. Travelers report their excursion, share minutes via online entertainment, and remain associated with the world past the train windows. The tracks become a channel for virtual investigation, as travelers bring the remarkable appeal of train travel to a worldwide crowd, making a local area of rail fans who praise the enchantment of the tracks.

The tracks likewise reverberation with the ecological difficulties related with train travel. The push for maintainable practices and eco-accommodating drives turns into a pivotal part of current rail line tasks. From energy-proficient trains to squander decrease endeavors, the tracks become a wilderness for developments that mean to limit the natural impression of train travel. The obligation to supportability changes the tracks into a pathway towards a greener and more capable future.

Chapter 6

The Dining Car Experience

The feasting vehicle experience unfurls as a charming story inside the moving bounds of a train, offering travelers food as well as an excursion into the domains of culinary pleasure, social collaboration, and an interesting mix of custom and development. The feasting vehicle, with its all encompassing windows outlining consistently evolving scenes, turns into a phase for gastronomic undertakings that rise above the simple demonstration of eating.

As travelers step into the eating vehicle, they are welcomed by a climate that weds tastefulness with the musical movement of the train. The curbed murmur of discussion, the ringing of cutlery, and the smell of newly pre-arranged dinners make a vivid feasting experience. The cautiously organized stylistic layout, frequently mirroring the appeal of a past period of extravagance train travel, adds a dash of sentimentality to the excursion.

The eating vehicle menu, a culinary embroidery woven by talented gourmet specialists, reflects the variety of the districts the train crosses. From neighborhood strengths to worldwide top picks, the menu turns into a gastronomic excursion that welcomes travelers to investigate the kinds of the objections outside their window. The test lies in offsetting experience with curiosity, guaranteeing that the eating vehicle turns into a mixture of tastes that take special care of a range of palates.

The culinary excursion inside the feasting vehicle isn't just about the objective; it's about the investigation of territorial cooking styles and the festival of nearby flavors. The storeroom vehicle staff and gourmet specialists curate menus that mirror the social embroidered artwork of the districts went through. An excursion across India, for instance, could include a culinary journey through the sweet-smelling flavors of the south, the rich Mughlai customs of the north, and the fish mixed pleasures of the waterfront locales.

The feasting vehicle turns into a center point for social collaboration, a space where outsiders become eating mates, sharing stories and giggling over a mutual dinner. The mutual eating experience cultivates a feeling of fellowship among travelers, separating social obstructions as they bond over a common appreciation for good food and the extraordinary experience of train travel. The clack of cutlery and the murmur of discussion become the soundtrack to these unconstrained associations framed in the core of the moving train.

Nonetheless, the eating vehicle experience reaches out past the mutual table, embracing the pattern of customized administration. Travelers, outfitted with computerized menus, practice their culinary inclinations, modifying their feasting experience to suit their preferences and dietary limitations. The feasting vehicle staff, skilled at exploring these customized demands, add an additional layer of individualization to the excursion, guaranteeing that every traveler's culinary inclinations are met with accuracy.

The culinary excursion inside the eating vehicle unfurls against the background of the train's musical development. The test for cooks and feasting vehicle staff lies in synchronizing dinner arrangement and administration with the train plan. The bound space requires fastidious preparation, with gourmet specialists arranging a culinary dance that adjusts to the rhythmic movement of the excursion. From the ringing of glasses during a toast to the introduction of each dish, each component of the feasting vehicle experience is finely tuned to the rhythm of the moving train.

The feasting vehicle turns into a material for culinary narrating, where each dish tells a story of nearby customs, verifiable impacts, and the culinary legacy of the locales served. A basic curry turns into a story of flavor shipping lanes, a pasta dish mirrors the Italian impacts on rail line catering, and a pastry grandstands the sweet customs of a specific objective. The feasting vehicle staff, knowledgeable in the accounts behind each dish, become culinary narrators, advancing the eating experience with social setting and authentic stories.

While the feasting vehicle experience praises the variety of local cooking styles, it additionally embraces the combination of customary and current culinary patterns. Culinary experts influence contemporary cooking methods to lift exemplary dishes, adding a layer of complexity to the installed eating experience. Sub-atomic gastronomy, sous-vide cooking, and other inventive techniques find their direction into the culinary collection of the feasting vehicle, guaranteeing that the excursion turns into a combination of immortal works of art and current gastronomic enjoyments.

The storage room vehicle, the culinary motor behind the eating vehicle experience, turns into a hive of imagination and accuracy. Cooks, frequently working in bound spaces, coordinate a culinary orchestra that changes crude fixings into culinary magnum opuses. The test lies in the readiness of dishes as well as in keeping up with the quality and newness of fixings in the midst of the imperatives of the moving train. The storeroom vehicle staff's capacity to explore these difficulties guarantees that the eating vehicle experience stays a sign of greatness.

The eating vehicle experience isn't just about the principal courses; it stretches out to the specialty of baked good, where treats become a sweet crescendo to the culinary orchestra. From provincial desserts that give recognition to nearby customs to debauched global sweets, the pastry menu turns into a grandstand of the different universe of candy parlor. The introduction of pastries is a work of art in itself, with every sweet creation adding a last dash of extravagance to the feasting experience.

Wine and spirits assume a significant part in improving the feasting vehicle experience, with cautiously organized refreshment menus supplementing the kinds of the dishes. The clunking of glasses and the nuanced specialty of wine matching hoist the feasting experience, transforming every dinner into a tactile excursion. The eating vehicle staff, knowledgeable in the subtleties of wine choice, guide travelers through an organized determination that upgrades the kinds of the culinary manifestations.

The eating vehicle is likewise a material for occasional and merry menus, changing the excursion into a festival of extraordinary events. Whether it's a merry banquet during occasions or a menu propelled by the evolving seasons, the feasting vehicle experience turns into a unique embroidery that develops with the schedule. Travelers end up submerged in an excursion that interfaces objections as well as imprints snapshots of festivity and social importance.

As the eating vehicle experience unfurls, it is interwoven with the strategic difficulties of train travel. The storage space vehicle staff and gourmet experts should adjust to the consistently changing storeroom of fixings accessible at different stops along the course.

Nearby business sectors become the wellspring of new produce, special flavors, and culinary motivation. The test lies in obtaining fixings as well as in adjusting to the irregularity and provincial subtleties that characterize the culinary scene.

The eating vehicle experience reaches out past the bounds of conventional feast administration, embracing the pattern of in and out choices. Travelers looking for a light meal or the people who like to eat in the protection of their lodges can browse a choice of tidbits and quick bites. The feasting vehicle staff's capacity to give a range of culinary choices guarantees that the eating experience takes care of the different inclinations and ways of life of travelers.

6.1 Evolution of dining car services on Indian trains

The development of eating vehicle administrations on Indian trains is a spellbinding excursion that traverses many years, mirroring the changing elements of movement, culinary inclinations, and mechanical headways. From humble starting points set apart by fundamental feast contributions to the cutting edge time portrayed by different menus, customized administrations, and the combination of conventional and contemporary culinary patterns, the eating vehicle experience on Indian trains has gone through a groundbreaking development.

In the beginning of train travel in India, eating on board was a simple undertaking. Fundamental dinners, frequently pre-stuffed and restricted in assortment, were served to travelers in basic feasting vehicles. The accentuation was on giving food as opposed to offering a culinary encounter. The eating vehicle, with its utilitarian methodology, was a practical space where travelers could get fundamental dinners during their excursion.

As train travel acquired fame and the interest for improved administrations developed, the Indian Rail lines perceived the need to raise the feasting experience. The primary critical jump in the development of eating vehicle administrations accompanied the presentation of on-board kitchens and storage room vehicles. Outfitted with cooking offices, these storage room vehicles considered the planning of newly prepared feasts, getting an undeniable improvement the quality and assortment of contributions.

The appearance of storage space vehicles worked with the presentation of local and different foods on trains. Travelers could now appreciate the kinds of various Indian states as the train crossed through differed scenes. The storage space vehicle turned into a culinary center on wheels, where gourmet specialists worked enthusiastically to create dinners that mirrored the rich embroidery of Indian culinary practices. This undeniable a critical shift from normalized, efficiently manufactured dinners to a more nuanced and regionalized eating experience.

The eating vehicle experience additionally developed with the presentation of feasting vehicles that took care of explicit classes of movement. While essential dinners stayed accessible for economy class travelers, the presentation of cooled and higher-class mentors carried with it a raised eating experience. Feasting vehicles intended for premium classes offered a more refined feel, customized administrations, and an extended menu, taking special care of the developing inclinations of knowing travelers.

The development of feasting vehicle administrations on Indian trains resembled the globalization of culinary patterns. The feasting vehicle menus started to consolidate global flavors and dishes, mirroring the changing sense of taste of a more cosmopolitan traveler base. Travelers could now enjoy various foods, from mainland treats to oriental joys, as the eating vehicle embraced a more diverse and comprehensive way to deal with its contributions.

The mechanical unrest in the 21st century assumed a crucial part in reshaping the feasting vehicle experience. The presentation of advanced menus, internet requesting frameworks, and credit only exchanges smoothed out the interaction, offering travelers more prominent comfort and productivity. Travelers could now scrutinize menus on their own gadgets, place orders carefully, and partake in a consistent feasting experience without the requirement for customary paper menus or money exchanges.

The eating vehicle experience likewise saw a shift towards more prominent personalization. Travelers, equipped with advanced menus and the capacity to modify their orders, could fit their eating experience to their particular inclinations. This shift from normalized dinners to customized decisions denoted a huge takeoff from the one-size-fits-all methodology of the past, mirroring an expanded accentuation on individual inclinations and dietary necessities.

The imbuement of innovation stretched out past the requesting system, arriving at the culinary heart of the excursion — the storeroom vehicle. Current kitchen gear, cutting edge cooking advancements, and effective stockpiling frameworks became fundamental to the storage space vehicle's tasks. The utilization of cutting edge cooking strategies, for example, sous-vide cooking and sub-atomic gastronomy, tracked down their direction into the culinary collection of storeroom vehicles, adding a contemporary style to customary top choices.

The feasting vehicle experience on Indian trains became an excursion of flavors as well as a festival of social variety. Extraordinary menu contributions during celebrations, provincial festivals, and critical events turned into a staple, permitting travelers to participate in the glad soul of social merriments even while progressing. This coordination of social festivals into the feasting vehicle experience added an additional layer of extravagance and social submersion to prepare travel.

The idea of superstar gourmet specialists and culinary coordinated efforts transformed the feasting vehicle experience, bringing a bit of marvelousness and skill to on-board dinners. Eminent cooks were roped in to organize unique menus, adding their particular dishes and culinary mastery to the train's contributions. These joint efforts raised the feasting vehicle experience, transforming it into a gastronomic experience organized by probably the most celebrated names in the culinary world.

The eating vehicle experience on Indian trains additionally embraced maintainability and eco-accommodating practices. Endeavors to limit squander, embrace harmless to the ecosystem bundling, and spotlight on privately obtained, occasional fixings became vital to the culinary ethos of train travel. The accentuation on manageability mirrored a more extensive cultural shift towards dependable and cognizant feasting rehearses.

Lately, the eating vehicle experience has turned into a point of convergence for development and variation. The difficulties presented by the Coronavirus pandemic provoked a reconsideration of cleanliness and security conventions, prompting the presentation of contactless feasting choices, upgraded sterilization measures, and a reestablished accentuation on food handling. The feasting vehicle experience turned into a demonstration of the business' strength even with phenomenal difficulties.

As the eating vehicle administrations on Indian trains keep on developing, the emphasis stays on making an all encompassing and noteworthy experience for travelers. The incorporation of innovation, the festival of different culinary practices, and the obligation to manageability highlight the feasting vehicle's change from a utilitarian space to a dynamic and fundamental part of the general train travel insight.

6.2 Luxurious and themed dining experiences offered

The domain of extravagant and themed feasting encounters on trains uncovers an entrancing embroidery of richness, development, and culinary imaginativeness. Past the traditional eating vehicle, certain trains all over the planet have raised the on-board culinary experience higher than ever, offering travelers a vivid excursion into the posh existence where each dinner turns into a festival of refined taste and guilty pleasure.

One of the zeniths of extravagance train travel is the celebrated Situate Express, a name inseparable from class and refinement. The feasting experience on the Orient Express isn't just about dinners; it is a dramatic situation, a presentation that unfurls in the luxuriously decorated eating vehicles suggestive of a past time. Precious stone ceiling fixtures, rich upholstery, and mindful help set up for a gastronomic excursion that reflects the glory of the train's celebrated history.

Themed feasting encounters on the Orient Express are a sign of its charm. From the English Pullman's rare carriages to the Venice Simplon-Situate Express' Craft Deco-enlivened feasting vehicles, each train inside the Orient Express family makes an unmistakable mood. Themed ventures, for example, the "English Pullman Murder Secret Lunch" or the "Venice Simplon-Situate Express Fabulous Suites," transport travelers to a period of charm and interest, transforming the eating vehicle into a phase for vivid narrating.

Rich trains like the Maharajas' Express in India rethink plushness on rails, offering a feasting experience that reflects the magnificence of illustrious royal residences. The feasting vehicles on the Maharajas' Express are decorated with choice craftsmanship, mirroring the rich social legacy of India's royal states. Travelers are blessed to receive a great gala, where the combination of customary Indian flavors with contemporary culinary strategies raises each feast to an imperial meal.

The Maharajas' Express goes past customary feasting, presenting themed culinary encounters that grandstand the assorted gastronomic practices of India. From the "Mayur Mahal" with its peacock-themed style to the "Rang Mahal" that praises the energetic shades of Indian flavors, each eating vehicle turns into a visual and gastronomic enjoyment. Themed suppers, for example, the "Safari Soiree" or the "Fortunes of India" exhibit the culinary wealth of the districts navigated, transforming the eating experience into a social investigation.

In Europe, the Regal Scotsman, one more embodiment of extravagance train travel, offers a feasting experience that joins the appeal of the Scottish Good countries with connoisseur guilty pleasure. The perception vehicle, with its all encompassing windows, gives a staggering scenery to dinners that include the best Scottish produce. From privately obtained fish to High country game, the Illustrious Scotsman's eating experience is a festival of Scotland's normal abundance.

Themed feasting encounters on the Imperial Scotsman incorporate excursions like the "Flavor of the High countries," where travelers set out on a culinary experience through Scotland's popular scenes. The train's yearly "Function Supper" hoists the feasting experience to a dark tie issue, complete with dazzling food, fine wines, and a dash of old-world marvelousness. These themed encounters change the eating vehicle into a setting for social drenching and culinary investigation.

Japan's Shiki-shima, an extravagance train that flawlessly mixes conventional craftsmanship with present day plan, rethinks the specialty of feasting on rails. The train's feasting vehicles highlight huge windows that outline the steadily changing scenes outside, making a quiet background for the culinary excursion. The utilization of neighborhood and occasional fixings guarantees that every dinner is an impression of Japan's rich culinary legacy.

Themed feasting encounters on Shiki-shima dig into the pith of Japanese style and culture. The "Rikyu" feasting vehicle, propelled by the renowned tea ace Sen no

Rikyu, offers a peaceful setting for kaiseki, a multi-course dinner that is a genuine tangible encounter. The "Miyabi" eating vehicle, with its rich plan and refined vibe, gives a scenery to connoisseur pleases that exhibit the quintessence of Japanese haute cooking. These themed eating encounters on Shiki-shima represent an amicable mix of custom and innovation.

The Blue Train in South Africa offers an eating experience that reflects the country's different scenes, from the bone-dry excellence of the Karoo to the lavish grape plantations of the Cape Winelands. The eating vehicle, with its sumptuous style and mindful help, turns into a phase for culinary greatness that features the kinds of South African cooking. Travelers are blessed to receive a gastronomic excursion that consolidates global culinary patterns with neighborhood fixings.

Themed feasting encounters on the Blue Train incorporate excursions like the "Go out on the town" course, where travelers appreciate the best South African wines matched with connoisseur cooking. The "Extravagance Golf Safari" joins an affection for golf with perfect eating, offering travelers a remarkable mix of donning experience and culinary guilty pleasure. These themed encounters change the eating vehicle into a powerful space that takes care of the shifted interests and inclinations of travelers.

The Rough Mountain dweller in Canada joins extravagance train travel with stunning landscape, offering a feasting experience that unfurls against the setting of the Canadian Rockies. The train's glass-domed eating vehicles give all encompassing perspectives on the normal marvels outside, making a feasting experience that submerges travelers in the untamed magnificence of the scenes. Privately propelled food, highlighting the best Canadian fixings, adds a particular flavor to the excursion.

Themed feasting encounters on the Rough Mountain dweller incorporate the "Excursion through the Mists Culinary Experience," where travelers leave on a gastronomic experience through the core of the Rockies. The "Main Section toward the West Culinary Investigation" exhibits the culinary customs of Western Canada, transforming the feasting vehicle into a phase for the district's different flavors. These themed ventures praise the culinary variety of Canada, offering travelers a vivid encounter that goes past conventional train eating.

The Ghan, a famous train that navigates the huge scenes of Australia, offers a feasting experience that catches the embodiment of the Outback. The Sovereign Adelaide Café on The Ghan turns into a culinary desert garden, serving connoisseur dinners propelled by the different districts the train crosses. From the lavish scenes of the Top Finish to the red deserts of Focal Australia, the feasting vehicle on The Ghan mirrors the changing tones and kinds of the Australian landmass.

Themed eating encounters on The Ghan incorporate the "Outback Voyager Supper," where travelers appreciate territorial fortes matched with fine Australian wines. The "Platinum Club" takes extravagance eating higher than ever, offering a cozy setting for connoisseur pleases that exhibit the culinary lavishness of Australia. These themed encounters change the eating vehicle into a gastronomic excursion that reflects the variety of the Australian scene.

The Venice Simplon-Situate Express, known for its ageless class, offers a famous feasting experience that transports travelers to the charm of the 1920s and 1930s. The feasting vehicles, with their Lalique glass boards and Workmanship Deco configuration, bring out a feeling of sentimentality and refinement. Travelers on the Venice Simplon-Situate Express are blessed to receive a culinary excursion that beholds back to the brilliant time of train travel.

Themed eating encounters on the Venice Simplon-Situate Express incorporate the "Paris to Istanbul" highway, an excursion that praises the notable course of the first Arrange Express. The "English Pullman" carriages, with their one of a kind appeal, offer themed encounters like the "Brilliant Period of Movement" venture, where travelers are shipped to a time of extravagance and refinement. These themed encounters transform the feasting vehicle into a period container, permitting travelers to remember the style of a past time.

In Asia, the Eastern and Oriental Express offers a feasting experience that consolidates the advantage of train travel with the culinary extravagance of Southeast Asia. The eating vehicles, embellished with exquisite wood framing and complex subtleties, make a refined setting for connoisseur dinners that grandstand the kinds of the district. Travelers leave on a culinary excursion that reflects the social variety of the scenes outside.

Themed eating encounters on the Eastern and Oriental Express incorporate the "Tales of the Promontory" venture, where travelers relish the culinary customs of Malaysia and Thailand. The "Eastern and Oriental Express Champagne Breakfast" adds a bit of guilty pleasure to morning dinners, transforming the eating vehicle into a scene for festivity. These themed encounters submerge travelers in the social and culinary woven artwork of Southeast Asia.

6.3 Passenger testimonials and memorable dining car moments

The inspiring stories and essential minutes shared by travelers on trains all over the planet illustrate the significant effect that eating vehicle encounters can have on the excursion. From captivating experiences with individual explorers to the disclosure of surprising culinary joys, traveler tributes offer a brief look into the rich embroidery of encounters that unfurl inside the bounds of the eating vehicle.

Travelers frequently relate the delight of fortunate associations made over shared dinners in the feasting vehicle. The common climate of the feasting vehicle, with its enticing tables and the clunking of cutlery, turns into an impetus for social connection. Outsiders become companions, and eating colleagues manufacture bonds that rise above the transient idea of train travel. These opportunity experiences, frequently prodded by a common appreciation for good food and the novel appeal of eating moving, become valued recollections that wait long after the excursion closes.

The variety of individual voyagers adds an additional layer of extravagance to the feasting vehicle experience. Travelers share accounts of drawing in discussions with individuals from various corners of the globe, each bringing an extraordinary viewpoint and social knowledge to the common table. The feasting vehicle turns into a mixture of dialects, customs, and foundations, cultivating a climate where the limits between outsiders disintegrate, giving way to a common feeling of kinship.

Vital minutes in the feasting vehicle frequently spin around the culinary enjoyments served ready. Travelers review the choice kinds of territorial foods, the imaginativeness of show, and the wonderful shocks that look for them in each course. Notable dishes, skillfully ready by installed gourmet specialists, become the stars of these stories, making a permanent imprint on the culinary recollections of the individuals who navigate the tracks.

Travelers much of the time share accounts of startling culinary revelations, where an opportunity choice from the menu acquaints them with another most loved dish. Whether a local specialty catches the embodiment of the objective or an imaginative creation that exhibits the gourmet expert's dominance, these culinary shocks add a component of energy to the feasting vehicle experience. The delight of culinary investigation turns into a common topic in traveler tributes, representing the ground-breaking force of a very much created feast.

The vibe of the feasting vehicle likewise assumes a critical part in molding important minutes for travelers. The rich style, mindful help, and the musical movement of the train outside the windows make a special setting that intensifies the eating experience. Travelers frequently offer thanks for the careful scrupulousness, whether it's the fresh table cloths, the glimmering silverware, or the encompassing lighting that makes way for a close and extraordinary dinner.

Themed eating encounters make a permanent imprint on the recollections of travelers who set out on these culinary excursions. Whether it's a one of a kind propelled soiree suggestive of the Brilliant Period of Movement or a happy festival that reflects the social extravagance of a particular district, themed eating encounters make a feeling of event and hoist the excursion past the normal. Travelers affectionately relate these themed experiences, where the feasting vehicle changes into a setting for social drenching, narrating, and gastronomic investigation.

Traveler tributes frequently reverberation the feeling that the feasting vehicle experience rises above the demonstration of eating; it turns into a tactile excursion that connects every one of the faculties. The delicate murmur of discussion, the ringing of glasses, and the fragrant ensemble of painstakingly made dishes add to a vivid encounter that stretches out past the limits of the eating vehicle. Travelers discuss the close to home reverberation of these minutes, where the culinary excursion turns into a string woven into the texture of their general travel insight.

In the domain of extravagance train travel, travelers share stories of unmatched guilty pleasure and complexity. The extravagant stylistic layout of the feasting vehicles, the mindful assistance, and the organized menus including the best fixings make a climate of richness that has a permanent effect. Traveler tributes from extravagance train travels frequently underline the groundbreaking idea of the feasting vehicle experience, where each dinner is a festival of refined taste and unmatched guilty pleasure.

Extraordinary events celebrated in the feasting vehicle become esteemed recollections for travelers. Whether it's an achievement birthday, a commemoration, or a heartfelt escape, the eating vehicle turns into a phase for private festivals. Travelers tell accounts of shock sweets, customized menus, and the acts of kindness of the feasting vehicle staff that add a hint of wizardry to these exceptional minutes. The feasting vehicle turns into a setting for making enduring recollections, where the delight of festivity is complicatedly woven into the texture of the excursion.

The visual scene outside the windows improves the feasting vehicle experience, making snapshots of stunningness and marvel. Travelers portray the stunning scenes that unfurl as the train winds its direction through mountains, valleys, and beautiful open country. The consistently changing perspectives add to the feeling of experience and disclosure, transforming each dinner in the feasting vehicle into a novel and vivid experience.

Traveler tributes likewise shed light on the job of the eating vehicle in encouraging a feeling of local area among voyagers. The common experience of eating on board makes a bond among travelers, who frequently end up trading travel stories, proposals, and tips. The feasting vehicle turns into a center point for social cooperation, where travelers from different foundations meet up to share dinners as well as the aggregate insight of train travel.

The effect of the eating vehicle experience reaches out past the actual excursion, impacting the manner in which travelers see train travel all in all. Numerous tributes express a freshly discovered appreciation for the sentiment, wistfulness, and sluggish speed of train travel. The feasting vehicle turns into an image of the novel appeal of crossing scenes by rail, where the excursion becomes as huge as the objections.

In snapshots of reflection, travelers frequently articulate the opinion that the eating vehicle experience typifies the substance of their train process. It turns into a microcosm of the bigger experience, a space where the social, culinary, and social elements of the movement experience unite. Traveler tributes act as a demonstration of the getting through charm of the eating vehicle, where each feast turns into a story, each experience a memory, and each excursion a remarkable section in the book of movement encounters.

Chapter 7

Catering to Diverse Palates

The craft of taking care of different palates on trains addresses a culinary odyssey that rises above geological limits, praising the rich embroidery of flavors that characterize worldwide food. As trains confound mainlands, catering administrations face the test of giving feasts that resound the different inclinations of travelers, offering a gastronomic excursion that reflects the social mosaic of the districts crossed.

One of the principal parts of taking special care of different palates is recognizing the multicultural structure of train voyagers. Travelers on trains hail from different foundations, carrying with them a range of tastes, dietary limitations, and culinary assumptions. The cooking administrations should explore this culinary variety with artfulness, guaranteeing that the installed menu is an agreeable mix of commonality and oddity, taking care of both the carefully prepared voyager and those setting out on their most memorable train venture.

Local variety is a critical thought in making menus that take care of a changed crowd. As trains navigate various states, regions, or nations, the culinary scene advances, introducing an open door to grandstand neighborhood claims to fame and bona fide flavors. Providing food administrations curate menus that give recognition to the culinary legacy of every district, permitting travelers to leave on a culinary excursion that reflects the changing scenes outside their window.

In India, eminent for its culinary variety, taking special care of different palates on trains is a perplexing dance of flavors and local rarities. From the fiery curries of the south to the fragrant biryanis of the north, Indian trains become moving exhibits of the country's rich gastronomic woven artwork. Catering administrations team up with nearby gourmet specialists to guarantee that the installed feasts truly address the kinds of the districts the train navigates, furnishing travelers with a culinary journey through the different culinary practices of India.

The idea of taking special care of different palates stretches out past public lines, finding reverberation in the globalized idea of train travel. Trains that cross global limits should explore the test of offering dinners that take care of the shifted preferences of a worldwide customers. The menus become a combination of global cooking styles, where travelers can relish Italian pasta one day, enjoy Japanese sushi the following, and experience the rich flavors of Indian curry on resulting ventures.

Obliging dietary inclinations and limitations is a critical part of taking care of different palates. Travelers might follow veggie lover, vegetarian, without gluten, or other particular eating regimens, requiring a smart way to deal with menu arranging. Catering administrations put resources into culinary imagination to guarantee that dietary inclinations are obliged as well as celebrated, with plant-based choices that rival their meat partners in flavor and show.

The catering business' responsiveness to the rising interest for better and more cognizant dietary patterns is apparent in the consideration of nutritious and economically obtained fixings in train menus. Travelers progressively look for dinners that line up with their health objectives, and catering administrations adapt to the situation by offering a scope of choices that focus on newness, quality, and nourishing equilibrium. From quinoa servings of mixed greens to plant-based protein options, the developing scene of train eating mirrors a more extensive cultural shift towards careful and wellbeing cognizant decisions.

Adjusting to the variety of present day palates likewise includes embracing culinary patterns and developments. Trains, once inseparable from customary solace food, are currently at the very front of gastronomic trial and error. Providing food administrations influence contemporary cooking strategies, for example, sous-vide cooking and sub-atomic gastronomy, to lift installed feasts to a degree of complexity that opponents fancy foundations.

Travelers find themselves fulfilled as well as pleased by the startling culinary turns that change train feasting into a culinary experience.

Personalization is a vital pattern in taking care of different palates, with innovation assuming a crucial part in furnishing travelers with adjustable eating encounters. Advanced menus, accessible on private gadgets, engage travelers to fit their dinners as per their inclinations. Whether it's changing flavor levels, settling on unambiguous fixings, or sticking to dietary limitations, the capacity to alter dinners upgrades the individualized idea of train travel.

Themed eating encounters, propelled by social celebrations, occasional festivals, or verifiable occasions, add an additional layer of variety to locally available catering. Travelers on themed ventures wind up drenched in a culinary story that goes past the standard menu, transforming the feasting vehicle into a phase for social investigation. From Christmas galas to Diwali festivities, themed eating encounters make a feeling of event and party, permitting travelers to participate in social customs while progressing.

Taking care of different palates includes a cautious thought of the social, strict, and dietary subtleties that characterize traveler inclinations. Halal and genuine feasts, for instance, are proposed to oblige the dietary necessities of explicit strict networks. The thoughtfulness regarding these subtleties mirrors a guarantee to inclusivity, guaranteeing that each traveler, no matter what their social foundation or dietary limitations, feels invited and took care of on their excursion.

The combination of customary and current culinary impacts is a sign of taking care of different palates. On trains, where sentimentality frequently interlaces with advancement, gourmet specialists draw motivation from both exemplary recipes and contemporary culinary patterns. The outcome is a menu that gives recognition to immortal top choices while embracing the developing preferences and inclinations of a cutting edge and knowing customer base.

Providing food administrations on trains likewise perceive the significance of connecting with travelers in the culinary experience past the feasting vehicle. Cooking shows, studios, and intuitive meetings with locally available gourmet experts give travelers experiences into the creativity behind their feasts. The straightforwardness in exhibiting the culinary cycle cultivates a more profound association among travelers and the food they devour, upgrading the general appreciation for the locally available eating experience.

In extravagance train travel, the obligation to taking care of different palates takes on an uplifted degree of refinement. The feasting vehicles on extravagance trains become culinary asylums, where Michelin-featured cooks curate menus that mirror an unflinching commitment to greatness. Travelers end up enjoying gastronomic spectacles, where each course is a show-stopper that rises above the conventional.

Wine and spirits assume a urgent part in supplementing the different flavors introduced on extravagance trains. Skillfully arranged wine records, highlighting vintages from prestigious grape plantations, improve the feasting experience, with sommeliers directing travelers through pairings that raise the kinds of each dish. The meticulousness in refreshment contributions reflects the general obligation to giving a complete and vivid culinary excursion.

Taking care of assorted palates isn't just about the dinners; about making a vibe improves the general feasting experience. The plan of the feasting vehicle, the nature of silverware, and the mindfulness of the help staff all add to the making of a noteworthy and charming space. The feasting vehicle turns into a safe house where travelers can unwind, interface with individual explorers, and enjoy each experience of their culinary excursion.

Traveler tributes frequently feature the snapshots of joy and astound that emerge from the endeavors to take care of different palates. The unforeseen disclosure of a provincial delicacy, the impeccably executed combination of flavors, or the customized regard for dietary inclinations become stories that travelers energetically share. These accounts, woven into the texture of the excursion, add to the aggregate story of the installed feasting experience.

7.1 Accommodating dietary preferences and restrictions

The scene of eating on trains has seen a change in perspective with a developing accentuation on obliging different dietary inclinations and limitations. As voyagers leave on train ventures for relaxation, business, or exceptional events, the catering business is entrusted with the test of giving feasts that take care of a range of dietary necessities, going from explicit culinary inclinations to different dietary limitations and sensitivities.

One of the vital changes in the domain of train feasting is the rising mindfulness and convenience of dietary inclinations. Travelers today carry various inclinations to the eating table, affected by elements like way of life decisions, social foundations, and individual wellbeing contemplations. Vegetarianism, veganism, and flexitarianism have become common dietary options, mirroring a more extensive cultural shift towards careful and purposeful eating.

Trains all over the planet are adjusting to these inclinations by integrating plant-based choices that go past conventional servings of mixed greens. Creative and tasty veggie lover and vegetarian dishes have become staples on train menus, offering travelers a different and fulfilling culinary experience. The culinary development stretches out to the show and imagination in plant-based contributions, scattering the thought that veggie lover or vegetarian feasts are restricted in assortment or flavor.

Adaptability in obliging dietary inclinations has turned into a sign of present day train eating administrations. Travelers are not generally restricted to unbending menu choices; all things being equal, they find a scope of decisions that take care of their singular preferences. From adjustable servings of mixed greens and sandwiches to plant-based protein choices, the capacity to fit dinners as per dietary inclinations has turned into a characterizing element of contemporary train eating.

The providing food industry's reaction to dietary inclinations isn't restricted to veggie lover and vegetarian decisions. The incorporation of without gluten, sans dairy, and other without allergen choices has turned into a need. Travelers with explicit dietary limitations or sensitivities presently have the confirmation that their dietary requirements will be met during their excursion. The careful thoughtfulness regarding fixing obtaining and planning procedures guarantees that dinners line up with tough dietary necessities without settling on flavor or quality.

Obliging dietary inclinations is especially apparent with regards to provincial and social varieties. As trains navigate different scenes and social areas, providing food administrations curate menus that celebrate neighborhood culinary customs. Travelers can enjoy credible territorial claims to fame that take care of different palates as well as give a vivid culinary encounter intelligent of the areas the train crosses.

The test of obliging dietary inclinations reaches out to global train travel, where travelers from different social foundations share common eating spaces. Trains crossing borders should explore the intricacy of assorted dietary standards and limitations, guaranteeing that dinners take special care of the preferences and inclinations of a worldwide customers. The outcome is a worldwide combination of flavors, where travelers can enjoy Italian pasta, Japanese sushi, Indian curry, or other global cooking styles, making a genuinely multicultural eating experience.

The ascent of innovation plays had a crucial impact in improving the experience of obliging dietary inclinations on trains. Computerized menus, open on private gadgets, engage travelers to survey and pick feasts in light of their dietary requirements. The consistent joining of innovation in the eating experience gives comfort as well as guarantees that travelers have a reasonable comprehension of the fixings utilized in each dish, working with informed decisions lined up with their inclinations.

Extravagance train travel takes the convenience of dietary inclinations higher than ever, where culinary greatness and personalization meet. Michelin-featured culinary experts on extravagance trains curate menus that rise above dietary limitations, offering a gastronomic excursion that matches the best eateries. The customized idea of extravagance train feasting permits travelers to impart their inclinations and dietary limitations ahead of time, guaranteeing that every dinner is a custom-made encounter.

Taking special care of different dietary inclinations additionally includes perceiving the social and strict aspects that impact travelers' culinary decisions. Prepares frequently give Halal and legitimate feast choices to take care of the dietary necessities of explicit strict networks. The incorporation of these choices mirrors a promise to inclusivity, guaranteeing that travelers from different social and strict foundations feel regarded and took care of during their excursion.

The culinary imagination showed in obliging dietary inclinations is obvious in the advancement of elective protein sources. Trains have embraced the pattern of consolidating plant-based protein options, like tofu, seitan, and vegetables, in creative and engaging ways. These choices take care of veggie lover and vegetarian inclinations as well as add to the more extensive development towards maintainable and moral eating rehearses.

Eating on trains has turned into a point of convergence for advancing wellbeing and health, lining up with the developing consciousness of the connection among diet and by and large prosperity. Cooking administrations are integrating nutritious and healthy choices into their menus, taking care of travelers looking for adjusted feasts that focus on newness, quality, and dietary benefit. From supplement rich plates of mixed greens to grain bowls and superfood-implanted dishes, the eating vehicle has turned into an objective for wellbeing cognizant voyagers.

Allergen mindfulness is a basic part of obliging dietary inclinations, as a developing number of travelers have food sensitivities or bigotries. Train providing food administrations focus on the security of travelers with sensitivities by carrying out thorough allergen the executives conventions. Clear naming, nitty gritty fixing data, and proactive correspondence among travelers and installed staff add to an eating climate where travelers with sensitivities can partake in their dinners with certainty.

The obligation to obliging dietary inclinations isn't just reflected in the menu decisions yet additionally in the preparation and consciousness of locally available staff. Culinary specialists and serving staff go through preparing to figure out the subtleties of various dietary inclinations and limitations. The capacity to give exact data, make reasonable suggestions, and address traveler questions in regards to dietary worries adds to an eating experience that isn't just heavenly yet in addition obliging and mindful of individual necessities.

Traveler tributes frequently feature the meaning of the endeavors made to oblige their dietary inclinations. Accounts of partaking in a connoisseur plant-based feast, relishing a sans gluten dessert, or valuing the mindfulness of obliging explicit dietary limitations are normal subjects in traveler stories. The regard for these subtleties makes a positive and noteworthy eating experience, adding to the general fulfillment of travelers during their excursion.

7.2 Special meal options and their popularity

The development of train feasting has seen a groundbreaking movement towards offering unique dinner choices that take special care of a range of dietary necessities, social inclinations, and culinary encounters. Extraordinary dinner choices have turned into a sign of current train travel, permitting travelers to customize their eating experience and guaranteeing that each excursion isn't simply a drive yet a culinary experience custom-made to individual preferences and necessities.

One of the critical drivers behind the ubiquity of exceptional feast choices is the rising variety of dietary inclinations among travelers. As people take on different dietary ways of life, including vegetarianism, veganism, sans gluten, and that's just the beginning, the interest for specific feasts has risen fundamentally. Train administrators and catering administrations have answered by growing their menu contributions to incorporate various exceptional feasts that line up with various dietary decisions, giving travelers choices that resound with their culinary qualities.

Veggie lover and vegetarian feast choices have become necessary to the unique dinner collection on trains, mirroring the worldwide flood in plant-based eating. Travelers settling on veggie lover or vegetarian dinners can now partake in a different exhibit of dishes that go past standard servings of mixed greens. Imaginative plant-based manifestations, wealthy in flavor and healthy benefit, have raised veggie lover and vegetarian eating on trains, drawing in not just those focused on a plant-based way of life yet additionally travelers inquisitive to investigate the dynamic universe of meatless cooking.

Sans gluten feast choices have acquired conspicuousness as attention to gluten awareness and celiac illness has expanded. Travelers requiring without gluten choices currently approach dinners that focus on sans gluten fixings and planning techniques. From sans gluten pasta to bread and sweets, the accessibility of these choices guarantees that people with gluten-related dietary limitations can partake in a protected and fulfilling feasting experience while ready.

Without allergen dinner choices have turned into a vital thought for travelers with food sensitivities. The careful treatment of allergens, clear naming, and concentrated dinner planning conventions add to a feasting climate where travelers with sensitivities can certainly partake in their feasts. Without allergen choices, which take care of normal allergens like nuts, dairy, and shellfish, grandstand a promise to traveler well-being and inclusivity.

The ubiquity of unique dinner choices isn't restricted to dietary contemplations alone; it stretches out to social and territorial inclinations too. As trains navigate different scenes and cross worldwide lines, cooking administrations have embraced the open door to exhibit the rich embroidered artwork of worldwide foods. Travelers can decide on extraordinary dinners that reflect explicit culinary customs, permitting them to leave on a gastronomic excursion that reflects the locales the train crosses.

Extraordinary feast choices additionally take care of travelers looking for better and lighter eating decisions. The accentuation on health and dietary equilibrium has prompted the consideration of extraordinary feasts that focus on new, healthy fixings. From supplement rich plates of mixed greens to incline protein choices, these dinners line up with the inclinations of wellbeing cognizant explorers, offering a culinary excursion that upholds their prosperity objectives.

The customization of dinner choices is a vital figure the notoriety of exceptional feasts. Travelers currently can fit their eating experience as per their particular preferences and inclinations. The presentation of computerized menus, open on private gadgets, enables travelers to survey and pick unique dinners in view of their dietary requirements, guaranteeing a consistent and customized eating experience that takes care of individual culinary inclinations.

In extravagance train travel, the ubiquity of unique dinner choices is enhanced, as these excursions are inseparable from richness and custom encounters. Michelin-featured cooks curate unique menus that take special care of the insightful preferences of extravagance train travelers. The capacity to convey inclinations and dietary prerequisites ahead of time permits travelers to partake in a feasting experience customized to their singular cravings, whether it be an exceptional festival or a longing for culinary excess.

Themed feasting encounters, frequently highlighting unique dinner choices, add an additional layer of appeal to prepare travel. Travelers on themed excursions can enjoy culinary festivals that concur with social celebrations, occasional occasions, or authentic achievements. Whether it's a Christmas feast, a Diwali festivity, or a connoisseur experience motivated by a particular district, themed eating encounters with extraordinary dinner choices make a feeling of event and merriment ready.

The ubiquity of exceptional dinner choices isn't exclusively determined by dietary limitations or inclinations; it is profoundly interlaced with the general eating experience on trains. Exceptional dinners add to the story of each excursion, transforming feasts into vital occasions that rise above simple food. Travelers share accounts of pleasure and fulfillment while finding a mindfully arranged exceptional feast that lines up with their preferences or dietary requirements, adding a positive and customized aspect to their movement recollections.

The meticulousness in unique dinner choices additionally reaches out to the culinary imagination showed in their show. Extraordinary dinners are not just about gathering dietary necessities; they are made to be outwardly engaging and tasty, guaranteeing that travelers infer both tangible delight and healthy benefit from their feasting experience. The creativity in unique feast readiness adds to a general feel of guilty pleasure and culinary refinement.

In the domain of extravagance train travel, unique dinner choices are raised to a fine art. Travelers can anticipate an unrivaled degree of customization, with the choice to team up with installed culinary specialists to make tailor made menus. Extraordinary feasts on extravagance trains go past gathering dietary necessities; they become impeccable culinary manifestations that mirror the exemplification of top notch food. From customized tasting menus to selective wine pairings, extravagance train eating is a demonstration of the marriage of culinary craftsmanship and individualized encounters.

The prominence of extraordinary feast choices is likewise powered by the business' obligation to supportability and moral eating. Trains have embraced the utilization of privately obtained, occasional, and economically delivered fixings in their extraordinary feast contributions. Travelers enthused about pursuing earth cognizant decisions can settle on dinners that line up with their qualities, adding to a feasting experience that mirrors a more extensive obligation to capable and careful eating rehearses.

The acknowledgment of the prevalence of extraordinary feast choices has provoked nonstop advancement in menu improvement. Providing food administrations and cooks on trains endeavor to keep up to date with developing dietary patterns, culinary inclinations, and health contemplations. The outcome is a dynamic and steadily extending collection of extraordinary feast choices that take special care of the different and developing preferences of travelers, guaranteeing that train eating stays a lively and vital piece of the general travel insight.

Traveler tributes frequently feature the positive encounters related with extraordinary dinner choices. Accounts of finding a delightful vegetarian dessert, enjoying a without gluten connoisseur dinner, or savoring a unique dish that reflects a territorial culinary custom are normal topics. The personalization and meticulousness in extraordinary feasts add to travelers' general fulfillment, transforming every dinner into a noteworthy and charming part of their train process.

7.3 Efforts to cater to international tastes on certain routes

The endeavors to take special care of worldwide preferences on specific train courses address a culinary undertaking that rises above borders, meaning to furnish travelers with a gastronomic excursion intelligent of worldwide variety.

As trains navigate global courses, the providing food industry faces the test of offering dinners that reverberate with the differed palates and social inclinations of a worldwide customers. These endeavors improve the eating experience on board as well as add to a feeling of social drenching, transforming every dinner into a culinary investigation of the districts the train navigates.

One of the characterizing elements of taking care of worldwide preferences on specific courses is the festival of worldwide foods. The menus on these trains become a material for exhibiting the rich embroidery of flavors from around the world. Travelers can set out on a culinary experience that reflects the social variety of the locales covered by the train venture. Whether it's relishing Italian pasta, getting a charge out of Japanese sushi, or enjoying Indian curry, the worldwide menu choices make a worldwide dining experience that catches the pith of every objective.

The consolidation of provincial claims to fame is a critical technique in taking care of global preferences. As trains crosscountry borders, catering administrations team up with nearby gourmet specialists and culinary specialists to arrange menus that feature credible flavors and customary dishes. Travelers can consequently encounter the culinary personality of every district, with extraordinary accentuation on neighborhood fixings, cooking methods, and social subtleties that characterize the gastronomic scene.

Endeavors to take special care of global preferences stretch out past simple menu expansion; they include a fastidious comprehension of social subtleties and culinary practices. Train providing food administrations put resources into examination and joint effort with culinary specialists to guarantee that the arrangement, show, and kinds of each dish line up with the credibility of the individual cooking styles. This meticulousness makes a vivid eating experience, permitting travelers to feel shipped to the core of the culinary customs they are inspecting.

Specialty feasting encounters themed around worldwide cooking styles add an additional layer of credibility and appeal to specific train courses. Travelers on these excursions can decide on themed dinners that reproduce the atmosphere and kinds of explicit districts or nations. From a French bistro setting to an Asian combination feast, themed eating encounters make a feeling of spot inside the limits of the feasting vehicle, permitting travelers to participate in social investigation through their culinary excursion.

The reconciliation of worldwide preferences isn't restricted to fundamental courses; it reaches out to treats, drinks, and tidbits. Travelers can enjoy a different exhibit of worldwide treats, from French cakes to Turkish joys, making a sweet end to their worldwide culinary excursion. Refreshment choices additionally mirror a worldwide pizazz, with arranged determinations of wines, spirits, and non-cocktails that supplement the different menu contributions.

Taking special care of global preferences includes adjusting to the assorted inclinations of travelers from various social foundations. Trains on worldwide courses frequently offer a scope of feast choices to take care of different dietary decisions, including veggie lover, vegetarian, sans gluten, and other specific weight control plans. The adaptability in menu arranging guarantees that each traveler, no matter what their culinary inclinations or limitations, can find a choice that lines up with their preferences, adding to a more comprehensive and pleasant eating experience.

Innovation assumes a pivotal part in upgrading the catering experience on trains with worldwide courses. Computerized menus, available on private gadgets, give travelers the accommodation of exploring and choosing their dinners ahead of time. The consistent joining of innovation guarantees that travelers have a reasonable comprehension of the global menu choices accessible to them, working with informed decisions and adding to a more customized eating venture.

In extravagance train travel, the endeavors to take special care of global preferences are raised to the apex of refinement. Michelin-featured cooks curate worldwide menus that rival the best eating foundations. The extravagance train experience turns into a culinary journey all over the planet, where each dish is a work of art intended to charm the most insightful palates. The custom idea of extravagance train eating permits travelers to convey their worldwide culinary inclinations, guaranteeing that every dinner is a customized experience that mirrors the embodiment of worldwide gastronomy.

Themed ventures that reflect notable global courses add to the endeavors to take special care of worldwide preferences. Travelers on these themed excursions can anticipate that menus that give proper respect should the culinary practices of the nations or areas being addressed. From the polish of European feasting on the Orient Express to the dynamic kinds of Southeast Asia on themed ventures, these encounters submerge travelers in the worldwide embroidery of tastes that characterize each course.

Joint efforts with eminent gourmet specialists and culinary powerhouses from various nations further improve the worldwide feasting experience on specific train courses. The ability and innovativeness of these culinary representatives add to the credibility and greatness of the global menu contributions. Travelers benefit from the culinary ability of incredibly famous gourmet experts, partaking in a feasting experience that mirrors the worldwide norm of gastronomic greatness.

Endeavors to take special care of global preferences likewise stretch out to the plan and mood of the eating vehicle. The stylistic layout, table settings, and generally speaking climate are arranged to inspire the social and stylish sensibilities of the districts being crossed. Travelers wind up drenched in a climate that transports them to various corners of the globe, making a feasting experience that isn't just delightful yet additionally outwardly and socially improving.

Traveler criticism and inclinations assume a significant part in forming the development of global menus on specific train courses. Catering administrations effectively look for input from travelers, lead reviews, and examine feasting patterns to grasp the changing scene of worldwide preferences. This unique criticism circle guarantees that the menus stay receptive to the developing culinary assumptions for travelers, adding to a feasting experience that is contemporary and intelligent of worldwide gastronomic patterns.

Endeavors to take special care of worldwide preferences on specific courses add to the general charm of train travel as a social and culinary excursion. The eating vehicle turns into a microcosm of the different scenes and flavors experienced during the train venture. Whether it's the zest implanted dishes of the Orient, the generous kinds of European cooking, or the sensitive nuances of Asian toll, the worldwide menu choices on specific train courses become a necessary piece of the movement account.

Chapter 8

Future Tracks

The fate of railroad providing food holds the commitment of groundbreaking advancements and outlook changes that will reclassify the culinary scene on trains. As innovation progresses, culinary inclinations develop, and maintainability turns into a focal concern, the rail line cooking industry is ready to embrace another time of feasting encounters. From upgraded digitalization to state of the art culinary strategies and an uplifted spotlight on manageability, what's to come tracks of rail route catering imagine an excursion that rises above customary limits and lifts the installed eating experience to exceptional levels.

One of the key directions forming the fate of railroad providing food is the coordination of cutting edge advanced innovations. Digitalization is set to alter the manner in which travelers draw in with menus, place orders, and redo their eating experience. Savvy, intelligent menus available through private gadgets will furnish travelers with definite data about the fixings, healthful substance, and readiness techniques for each dish. The consistent mix of innovation won't just improve the general feasting experience yet additionally enable travelers to pursue educated and customized decisions.

The fate of rail route providing food imagines the far and wide reception of man-made consciousness (simulated intelligence) and AI to dissect traveler inclinations and patterns. Man-made intelligence calculations will use information on past feasting decisions, dietary limitations, and criticism to organize customized menu proposals for individual travelers. This degree of customization guarantees that every traveler's culinary excursion lines up with their inclinations, making a feasting experience that feels custom-made to their interesting preferences.

Virtual and expanded reality (VR and AR) advancements are ready to assume an extraordinary part coming soon for installed eating. Travelers can utilize VR head-sets to leave on virtual culinary excursions, investigating the starting points of fixings, seeing the planning system, and in any event, collaborating with eminent gourmet experts. AR overlays on feasting tables could give vivid data about the dishes being served, making a multi-tactile encounter that goes past taste and stretches out to visual and educational aspects.

The joining of innovation reaches out to the kitchen also, with the future seeing the far and wide utilization of mechanization and mechanical technology. Mechanized cooking processes, mechanical culinary specialists, and savvy kitchen machines will smooth out food arrangement, guaranteeing proficiency and accuracy in the kitchen. This tends to calculated difficulties as well as permits culinary groups to zero in on imagination and development, prompting a better quality of value in locally available dinners.

Supportability is a foundation representing things to come tracks of railroad providing food, mirroring the business' obligation to natural obligation. From obtaining privately created, occasional fixings to limiting food squander through proficient stock administration, manageability practices will be implanted in each part of the cooking system. Trains are supposed to take on eco-accommodating bundling, execute reusing programs, and investigate elective energy hotspots for kitchen tasks, adding to a more practical and eco-cognizant eating experience.

The idea of homestead to-prepare will acquire noticeable quality later on, with providing food administrations laying out direct organizations with nearby ranchers and makers. This guarantees the newness and nature of fixings while decreasing the carbon impression related with transportation. Travelers can expect a homestead to-table insight ready, enjoying dishes made from privately obtained, feasible fixings that mirror the culinary personality of the locales the train crosses.

What's in store tracks of rail line cooking will observer a development of plant-based and elective protein choices to take care of the developing interest for veggie lover and vegetarian dinners.

Culinary imagination will be released to foster plant-based dishes that rival their meat partners in flavor, surface, and dietary benefit. The attention on plant-driven menus lines up with worldwide patterns advancing cognizant and feasible eating works on, furnishing travelers with different and fulfilling choices.

In the time of hyper-personalization, the eventual fate of rail line cooking will focus on individualized eating encounters. Travelers will can modify their feasts in light of individual inclinations, dietary limitations, and nourishing objectives. The utilization of innovation, including portable applications and installed interfaces, will work with consistent correspondence among travelers and providing food administrations, taking into consideration ongoing customization and guaranteeing that each dinner is an impression of the traveler's interesting preferences.

Culinary the travel industry on trains will turn into a critical pattern from here on out, with trains offering organized ventures based on gastronomic investigation. Themed culinary encounters, like celebrate visits, territorial cooking exhibits, and gourmet specialist drove culinary undertakings, will draw in travelers looking for a more vivid and liberal travel insight. These culinary excursions won't just commend the variety of flavors yet additionally grandstand the social and culinary legacy of the locales covered by the train courses.

Extravagance train head out is ready to arrive at new levels from here on out, with an accentuation on unmatched culinary greatness. Michelin-featured culinary specialists and gastronomic specialists will assume a necessary part in forming the feasting encounters on extravagance trains. Travelers can anticipate tailor made menus, selective wine pairings, and connoisseur feasting that equals the best eateries. The combination of extravagance, culinary creativity, and customized administration will characterize the encapsulation of extravagance train feasting.

The idea of spring up eateries on trains will arise as a dynamic and imaginative pattern from here on out. Trains might team up with eminent gourmet experts, neighborhood culinary gifts, and spring up eating ideas to present restricted time, selective feasting encounters ready. These spring up eateries will bring a feeling of curiosity and energy to prepare travel, offering travelers the potential chance to enjoy novel and moving culinary manifestations.

In light of the rising significance of wellbeing and wellbeing cognizant feasting, the eventual fate of railroad catering will see an extension of supplement rich and careful menu choices. Superfood-injected dishes, adjusted dinner plans, and wellbeing focused feasting encounters will take care of travelers looking for nutritious and healthy dinners. The combination of healthful data into menu depictions will engage travelers to pursue decisions lined up with their prosperity objectives.

Joint efforts with superstar gourmet specialists, culinary powerhouses, and food specialists will be a conspicuous element representing things to come of rail route catering. Trains will have extraordinary culinary occasions, studios, and intuitive meetings where travelers can draw in with culinary characters, find out about assorted foods, and gain bits of knowledge into the specialty of gastronomy. These coordinated efforts will improve the general feasting venture, making essential and instructive encounters for travelers.

Endeavors to limit the ecological effect of railroad providing food will stretch out to squander decrease drives. Trains will carry out imaginative answers for limit food squander, like shrewd dividing, treating the soil projects, and associations with nearby food banks. The obligation to squander decrease lines up with more extensive maintainability objectives, guaranteeing that the culinary excursion on trains isn't just delightful yet additionally naturally mindful.

Local area commitment will be a point of convergence representing things to come of rail route cooking, with trains interfacing with nearby networks to improve the installed feasting experience. Joint efforts with nearby craftsmans, food makers, and social associations will bring about extraordinary and true culinary contributions. Travelers can expect a more vivid and socially enhancing eating venture that encourages an association between the train and the networks it navigates.

What's in store tracks of rail route cooking will see an expanded accentuation on food style and show. Culinary groups will investigate creative plating methods, imaginative toppings, and outwardly staggering dish structures. The objective is to hoist the eating experience past taste, making a banquet for the eyes and upgrading the generally tangible delight of installed feasts. The combination of culinary imaginativeness and visual allure will reclassify the style of train eating.

The presentation of shrewd feasting vehicles later on will change the general eating mood on trains. Shrewd lighting, intuitive showcases, and versatile guest plans will add to a dynamic and customized feasting climate. Travelers can expect a tangible rich encounter where the climate adjusts to the hour of day, the view outside, and the temperament of the excursion, upgrading the general satisfaction in installed feasts.

As the fate of rail route providing food unfurls, the business will keep on embracing social variety and inclusivity. Endeavors to take special care of worldwide preferences will be enhanced, with menus mirroring the worldwide culinary mosaic. Trains on global courses will offer a variety of dishes that feature the bona fide flavors and culinary customs of every nation, guaranteeing that travelers experience a genuine taste of the world during their excursion.

8.1 Innovations in railway catering technology and services

Developments in railroad catering innovation and administrations are forming another period of locally available feasting encounters, reclassifying the manner in which travelers connect with menus, request dinners, and draw in with culinary contributions during their train processes. As innovation progresses, the railroad cooking industry is utilizing state of the art developments to upgrade proficiency, further develop consumer loyalty, and make a consistent and customized feasting experience for travelers.

One of the key mechanical advancements changing rail route providing food is the mix of savvy and intelligent menus. Computerized menus open through private gadgets, for example, cell phones or tablets, are turning into a typical element on present day trains. Travelers can peruse an outwardly engaging and easy to use interface, investigating a thorough scope of menu choices with definite depictions, pictures, and wholesome data. This smoothes out the requesting system as well as gives travelers a more vivid and informed feasting experience.

The reception of computerized reasoning (man-made intelligence) and AI (ML) is reforming menu personalization and proposal frameworks. Simulated intelligence calculations examine traveler inclinations, past orders, and segment information to propose custom fitted menu choices. This degree of personalization guarantees that travelers get menu suggestions lined up with their singular preferences and dietary inclinations, adding to an additional client driven and charming feasting venture.

Portable applications committed to rail route catering are acquiring ubiquity, permitting travelers to helpfully peruse menus, place requests, and make secure installments from their cell phones. These applications frequently offer elements like continuous following of requests, customized advancements, and the capacity to give criticism on the feasting experience. The coordination of versatile applications smoothes out the whole catering process, giving travelers an easy to understand and productive stage to deal with their installed eating inclinations.

The utilization of contactless innovation is turning out to be progressively pervasive in railroad providing food, particularly in light of general wellbeing contemplations. Contactless installment choices, for example, versatile installment stages and contactless cards, offer a safe and clean way for travelers to settle their feasting bills without actual contact. This development lines up with the advancing assumptions for a touchless and consistent travel insight, adding to the general security and prosperity of travelers.

Increased reality (AR) is making advances into the rail line catering space, upgrading the manner in which travelers draw in with menus and locally available feasting. AR applications can overlay advanced data onto the actual climate, permitting travelers to see virtual portrayals of menu things, access extra insights regarding fixings, and even imagine the introduction of dishes on their table. This vivid utilization of AR adds a novel and intelligent aspect to the eating experience.

Robotized candy machines and booths at train stations are arising as helpful answers for take special care of travelers' nearby culinary necessities. These machines offer a scope of bites, drinks, and pre-bundled dinners, furnishing travelers with speedy and open choices prior to boarding or during short stops. The combination of candy machines improves the accessibility of food decisions, taking special care of fluctuating inclinations and timetables.

The Web of Things (IoT) is assuming a groundbreaking part in improving functional effectiveness and client care in rail line cooking. IoT-associated gadgets in kitchens and feasting vehicles empower continuous observing of stock levels, hardware status, and food temperatures. This proactive checking guarantees opportune recharging of provisions, limits wastage, and keeps up with the quality and security of installed dinners. Also, IoT sensors can add to prescient support, diminishing the gamble of hardware disappointments and administration interruptions.

The idea of brilliant feasting vehicles is building up some forward movement, where innovation is utilized to establish an insightful and versatile eating climate. Brilliant lighting, temperature control, and general media frameworks can be changed in view of variables like the hour of day, the picturesque environmental elements, and the mind-set of the excursion. This makes a dynamic and customized climate in the feasting vehicle, upgrading the by and large tangible experience for travelers.

Blockchain innovation is being investigated as an answer for upgrade straightforwardness and discernibility in the store network of food fixings. By executing blockchain, the whole excursion of fixings - from obtaining to conveyance - can be recorded and checked. This not just guarantees the realness and nature of the fixings yet in addition adds to building trust among travelers with respect to the obtaining and treatment of food items.

Improved information investigation abilities are engaging railroad cooking administrations to acquire further experiences into traveler inclinations, feasting patterns, and functional efficiencies. Investigating huge datasets permits catering suppliers to pursue information driven choices, streamline menu contributions, and designer administrations to meet advancing traveler assumptions. This information driven approach adds to a more responsive and client centered cooking biological system.

The eventual fate of rail route catering might observer the presentation of savvy kitchen hardware and machines that influence trend setting innovations. From insightful preparing apparatuses to computerized food readiness frameworks, these developments mean to smooth out kitchen tasks, decrease physical work, and upgrade the general proficiency of installed culinary administrations. The incorporation of savvy kitchen innovations can add to a more predictable and great feasting experience for travelers.

In the domain of extravagance train travel, virtual attendant services are being investigated to lift the general traveler experience. Through virtual attendant stages, travelers can get to customized feasting suggestions, make tailor made menu demands, and get constant help with their culinary inclinations. This degree of customized administration adds a dash of selectiveness and refinement to extravagance train feasting, taking special care of the insightful preferences of top of the line explorers.

Biometric confirmation advancements are being investigated to upgrade the security and proficiency of installed providing food administrations. Biometric frameworks can be carried out for secure admittance to eating regions, customized dinner suggestions in light of individual biometric information, and smoothed out registration processes. The mix of biometrics adds to a consistent and secure feasting experience for travelers.

Because of the rising interest for feasible practices, rail route catering administrations are investigating eco-accommodating bundling arrangements. Biodegradable materials, recyclable bundling, and reusable holders are being taken on to limit the natural effect of installed feasting. These drives line up with more extensive manageability objectives, adding to the decrease of single-use plastics and advancing eco-cognizant decisions among travelers.

The future of installed diversion and eating intermingling is turning into a reality with coordinated sight and sound encounters. Shrewd feasting tables outfitted with intelligent presentations can give travelers diversion choices, data about menu things, and, surprisingly, virtual culinary encounters. This union of eating and diversion changes the feasting vehicle into a multifunctional space, improving the general traveler experience.

Voice-enacted innovation is advancing into rail line catering, permitting travelers to put orders, alter inclinations, and cooperate with installed eating administrations through voice orders. Voice-enacted collaborators can give sans hands command over advanced menus, making it more advantageous for travelers to explore choices and spot orders without the requirement for actual cooperation with gadgets. This development takes care of the developing interest for instinctive and open innovation arrangements.

The joining of continuous input frameworks permits travelers to share their feasting encounters quickly. Advanced input stages empower travelers to give remarks, evaluations, and ideas, assisting providing food administrations with measuring consumer loyalty and recognize regions for development. This iterative criticism circle adds to consistent refinement of administrations, guaranteeing that the developing inclinations and assumptions for travelers are tended to immediately.

Expanded reality (AR) and computer generated reality (VR) are being investigated as devices to improve the general eating climate on trains. AR applications can overlay advanced upgrades onto the actual feasting climate, making virtual components that supplement the subject or environment of the excursion. VR encounters can ship travelers to virtual feasting settings, submerging them in a visual and hear-able excursion that supplements their culinary experience.

As railroad cooking innovation propels, network safety measures are essential to shield traveler information, installment data, and functional frameworks. Vigorous network safety conventions, including encryption, secure installment passages, and standard framework reviews, are basic to safeguard against potential digital dangers and guarantee the classification and respectability of locally available catering administrations.

8.2 Sustainability initiatives in food packaging and sourcing

Manageability drives in food bundling and obtaining address a basic part of the more extensive development towards earth dependable practices inside the food business. As worries about environmental change, plastic contamination, and asset consumption strengthen, organizations across the food store network are progressively zeroing in on feasible answers for limit their natural effect. From imaginative bundling materials to moral obtaining rehearses, these drives are reshaping how food is delivered, bundled, and devoured, encouraging a more manageable and dependable way to deal with the worldwide food framework.

One of the essential areas of concentration in maintainability drives is the decrease of single-use plastics in food bundling. The inescapable utilization of plastic bundling has contributed altogether to natural contamination, with plastic waste hurting biological systems, marine life, and human wellbeing. Accordingly, the food business is effectively investigating elective materials that are biodegradable, compostable, or effectively recyclable. Developments in plant-based plastics, biodegradable movies, and compostable bundling are building up some decent momentum, giving eco-accommodating options in contrast to customary plastic bundling.

Bioplastics, got from inexhaustible assets like cornstarch, sugarcane, or green growth, are arising as a reasonable option in contrast to traditional petrol based plastics. These biodegradable materials offer comparable usefulness to conventional plastics yet have an essentially lower natural effect. Producers and bundling organizations are progressively consolidating bioplastics into their bundling arrangements, addressing worries about plastic contamination and adding to a more round and economical economy.

The idea of zero-squander bundling is picking up speed, meaning to dispose of or limit bundling waste all through the whole life pattern of an item. This includes overhauling bundling to be all the more effectively recyclable, advancing reusable bundling choices, and empowering shoppers to take on reasonable removal rehearses. Zero-squander bundling drives diminish ecological effect as well as resound with purchasers who are progressively looking for items lined up with their upsides of natural stewardship.

The shift towards reasonable bundling reaches out to the inexpensive food and café industry, where single-use bundling has been a huge supporter of waste. Drives to supplant plastic straws with paper or reusable other options, offer fixings in biodegradable sachets, and utilize compostable holders for takeout dinners are turning out to be more boundless. The obligation to practical bundling in the foodservice area mirrors a more extensive familiarity with the business' part in diminishing its natural impression.

Moral and supportable obtaining of fixings is one more urgent component of maintainability drives in the food business. Purchasers are progressively worried about the social and natural effect of food creation, provoking an interest for straightforwardness and responsibility in the obtaining practices of food organizations. Maintainable obtaining envelops contemplations, for example, fair work rehearses, biodiversity protection, and the in general environmental impression of the production network.

Certificate programs, for example, Fair Exchange and Rainforest Coalition, assume a crucial part in confirming and advancing moral obtaining rehearses. These certificates guarantee that food items are obtained from makers who stick to social and ecological principles, including fair wages, safe working circumstances, and earth maintainable horticultural practices. The unmistakable quality of such affirmations on food bundling signs to shoppers that the item lines up with moral and feasible obtaining standards.

Nearby obtaining is acquiring ubiquity as a maintainable practice that diminishes the carbon impression related with shipping food over significant distances. Eateries, general stores, and food makers are progressively focusing on nearby ranchers and providers to help provincial economies and diminish the natural effect of food transportation. This shift towards nearby obtaining adds to supportability objectives as well as cultivates a feeling of local area and association among makers and shoppers.

Regenerative horticulture is arising as an all encompassing way to deal with practical cultivating that expects to reestablish and improve biological system wellbeing. Dissimilar to regular cultivating rehearses that might exhaust soil fruitfulness and add to ecological corruption, regenerative agribusiness centers around further developing soil wellbeing, expanding biodiversity, and sequestering carbon. By advancing regenerative practices, the food business can assume a part in moderating environmental change and supporting reasonable land the executives.

The reception of roundabout economy standards is reshaping the food business' way to deal with obtaining and squander the executives. In a roundabout economy, assets are utilized productively, and squander is limited through practices like reusing, upcycling, and treating the soil. Organizations are investigating ways of making shut circle frameworks where squander from one phase of the production network turns into a significant contribution for another. This approach lessens the natural effect as well as advances a more practical and tough food framework.

Bundling advancements that focus on recyclability and material proficiency are fundamental to manageability drives. The improvement of mono-material bundling, which comprises of a solitary sort of material that is effectively recyclable, works on the reusing system and diminishes the probability of bundling winding up in land-fills. Moreover, lightweighting - the act of involving less material in bundling without undermining its trustworthiness - adds to asset productivity and a lower carbon impression.

The upcycling of food results is acquiring consideration as a manageable answer for limit squander in the food store network. By changing food squander into significant items, like elements for new food items or bio-based materials, organizations can remove extra worth from assets that sounds disposed of, really. Upcycling lines up with the standards of a round economy and adds to more manageable and asset proficient food creation.

Innovation is assuming a crucial part in propelling manageability drives in food ob-taining and bundling. Blockchain innovation, for example, empowers straightforward and discernible stock chains, permitting buyers to follow the excursion of their food items from ranch to table. This straightforwardness cultivates trust and responsibility in the obtaining system, guaranteeing that moral and feasible practices are stuck to all through the production network.

Man-made brainpower (simulated intelligence) is being utilized to advance store network the executives, decrease food waste, and improve asset productivity. Artificial intelligence calculations break down information on variables, for example, request guaging, stock administration, and transportation coordinated factors to smooth out activities and limit ecological effect. By tackling the force of information and prescient investigation, organizations can settle on informed choices that line up with manage-ability objectives.

Cooperative drives between food organizations, government bodies, and non-legislative associations (NGOs) are driving fundamental change in the business. Orga-nizations that advance economical obtaining rehearses, advocate for strategy changes, and offer help for limited scope ranchers add to an aggregate work to fabricate a more maintainable and versatile food framework. These joint efforts influence the qualities of different partners to address complex difficulties and drive positive change.

Customer training and mindfulness crusades assume a urgent part in empowering manageable utilization designs. Food organizations are progressively straightforward about their maintainability drives, sharing data on bundling decisions, obtaining rehearses, and ecological responsibilities with purchasers. By enabling customers with information, organizations can cultivate a feeling of shared liability regarding manage-ability and empower informed decisions.

Unofficial laws and strategies are instrumental in forming the scene of supportability in food bundling and obtaining. As familiarity with ecological issues develops, states are carrying out measures to boost reasonable practices and beat naturally destructive ones down. Strategies like expanded maker obligation (EPR) and plastic boycotts add to an administrative system that lines up with maintainability objectives and urges organizations to take on eco-accommodating practices.

Purchaser interest for reasonable items and practices is a main thrust behind the reception of supportability drives in the food business. Organizations are answering the inclinations of naturally cognizant buyers by integrating manageability into their image character, promoting procedures, and item contributions. The force of shopper decision impacts organizations to focus on maintainability, making a market-driven shift towards more eco-accommodating practices.

8.3 Predictions and possibilities for the future of Indian railway catering

The fate of Indian rail route providing food holds a plenty of forecasts and con-ceivable outcomes, driven by mechanical headways, changing purchaser inclinations, and a developing accentuation on manageability. As we imagine the direction of rail line catering in India, a few vital patterns and potential outcomes arise, promising to rethink the culinary excursion for a large number of travelers navigating the huge rail line organization.

Digitalization is set to assume a urgent part in forming the fate of Indian rail line cooking. The boundless reception of advanced stages and versatile applications will change the manner in which travelers associate with menus, place orders, and alter their eating experience.

Savvy menus available through private gadgets will furnish travelers with point by point data about the different culinary contributions, working with educated and customized decisions. The combination of man-made consciousness (simulated intelligence) and AI (ML) will additionally improve the traveler experience by giving customized menu suggestions in view of individual inclinations and past eating history.

Increased reality (AR) and computer generated reality (VR) advancements will add a vivid layer to the feasting experience on Indian trains. Travelers might utilize AR applications to investigate virtual portrayals of dishes, view data about fixings, and even participate in intuitive culinary encounters. VR encounters could ship travelers to virtual feasting settings, giving a multisensory venture that supplements the kinds of the installed dinners. These advances won't just raise the feasting feeling yet in addition add to the general delight in the culinary excursion.

Manageability will be a foundation representing things to come of Indian railroad catering, mirroring a worldwide shift towards eco-accommodating practices. The de-crease of single-use plastics, imaginative bundling arrangements, and an emphasis on neighborhood and occasional obtaining will become necessary to the catering scene.

Trains might take on biodegradable and compostable bundling materials, lining up with the more extensive objective of limiting the ecological effect of locally available eating. The reconciliation of maintainable practices won't just enticement for earth cognizant travelers yet in addition add to India's obligation to eco-accommodating drives.

Neighborhood and provincial flavors will become the overwhelming focus coming down the line for Indian rail route cooking. Trains will progressively feature the rich and various culinary legacy of various states and areas. Travelers can expect a culinary excursion that praises the legitimate kinds of neighborhood cooking styles, offering a sample of the social embroidery that characterizes every district. This accentuation on local variety won't just upgrade the gastronomic experience yet in addition encourage a feeling of social investigation for travelers.

Extravagance train head out is ready to arrive at new levels in India, with an emphasis on unrivaled culinary greatness. Michelin-featured cooks and famous culinary specialists might team up with rail line catering administrations to arrange restrictive and connoisseur menus for extravagance trains. Travelers on these superior excursions can expect tailor made feasting encounters, wine pairings, and gastronomic joys that rival the best eateries. The combination of extravagance, culinary masterfulness, and customized administration will characterize the encapsulation of extravagance train eating in India.

Culinary the travel industry will turn into a critical pattern, with trains offering organized ventures revolved around gastronomic investigation. Themed culinary encounters, for example, food and wine visits, local cooking grandstands, and gourmet expert drove culinary undertakings, will draw in travelers looking for a more vivid and liberal travel insight.

These culinary excursions will grandstand the variety of Indian cooking as well as feature the special kinds of various states and districts covered by the train courses.

Plant-based and reasonable menu choices will observer a flood in fame as the interest for vegan and eco-accommodating decisions develops. Rail route catering administrations will grow their contributions to incorporate imaginative and tasty plant-based dishes, taking special care of the inclinations of wellbeing cognizant and ecologically mindful travelers. The joining of assorted veggie lover and vegetarian choices won't just line up with worldwide food drifts yet in addition take special care of the different dietary selections of travelers.

Coordinated efforts with VIP gourmet specialists, culinary powerhouses, and nearby food craftsmans will turn into a noticeable element of Indian rail route cooking. Trains might have extraordinary culinary occasions, studios, and intelligent meetings where travelers can draw in with culinary characters, find out about assorted cooking styles, and gain experiences into the specialty of gastronomy. These joint efforts won't just upgrade the feasting experience yet additionally make noteworthy and instructive minutes for travelers.

The presentation of savvy eating vehicles is not too far off, reforming the general feasting atmosphere on Indian trains. Shrewd lighting, intelligent presentations, and versatile guest plans will add to a dynamic and customized feasting climate. Travelers can expect a tactile rich encounter where the environment adjusts to the hour of day, the grand environmental factors, and the temperament of the excursion, upgrading the general delight in installed dinners.

Development in menu arranging and food readiness will be driven by a pledge to quality and effectiveness. High level kitchen gear, computerization, and brilliant apparatuses will smooth out the cooking processes, guaranteeing steady and great feasts even at scale. The culinary groups liable for rail line providing food will embrace innovation to beat strategic difficulties and spotlight on inventive menu arranging that features the wealth of Indian cooking.

Neighborhood and distinctive joint efforts will turn into a characterizing component of Indian rail route cooking, interfacing trains with the culinary practices of the districts they cross. Organizations with nearby ranchers, makers, and craftsmans will guarantee the utilization of new and legitimate fixings, adding to the financial prosperity of neighborhood networks. Travelers can expect a culinary excursion that charms their taste buds as well as supports the manageable development of neighborhood food environments.

Endeavors to limit food waste will be a key concentration, with trains carrying out inventive arrangements like brilliant partitioning, fertilizing the soil projects, and joint efforts with neighborhood food banks.

The obligation to squander decrease lines up with more extensive manageability objectives, guaranteeing that the culinary excursion on Indian trains isn't just heavenly yet additionally ecologically dependable. Travelers can anticipate that a more honest methodology should food planning and utilization, adding to the decrease of food squander across the rail line catering industry.

Mechanical progressions will stretch out to the strategies of flavor, with the execution of brilliant stock administration frameworks and ongoing following of fixings. This guarantees that kitchens are all around supplied with new and great fixings, limiting the gamble of deficiencies and upgrading the general effectiveness of the cooking system. The operations of flavor will turn into a consistent and mechanically determined part of rail route cooking, ensuring a reliable and brilliant feasting experience for travelers.

Local area commitment will be a point of convergence, with trains interfacing with nearby networks to improve the installed eating experience. Coordinated efforts with neighborhood craftsmans, food makers, and social associations will bring about extraordinary and real culinary contributions. Travelers can expect a more vivid and socially improving feasting venture that encourages an association between the train and the different networks it navigates.

The incorporation of voice-enacted innovation will furnish travelers with a sans hands and instinctive method for interfacing with installed feasting administrations.

Voice-enacted associates might help travelers in setting orders, altering inclinations, and getting to data about the menu. This advancement takes special care of the developing assumptions for travelers for consistent and easy to use cooperations, making the eating experience more open and helpful.

Endeavors to take special care of different dietary inclinations and limitations will be enhanced, with an emphasis on giving comprehensive menu choices. Trains will offer a scope of decisions for travelers with explicit dietary requirements, including sans gluten, sans nut, and without allergen choices. The obligation to obliging different dietary inclinations mirrors a client driven approach, guaranteeing that each traveler can partake in a fantastic and comprehensive feasting experience.

Developments in food transportation and safeguarding techniques will improve the quality and newness of locally available feasts. From cutting edge refrigeration frameworks to eco-accommodating bundling arrangements, these developments will add to a more supportable and effective production network. Travelers can expect a consistent and solid transportation of fixings, guaranteeing that the kinds of local cooking styles are saved and celebrated all through the excursion.

The presentation of themed feasting encounters will add a novel and engaging aspect to Indian rail line catering. Trains might have themed occasions, like bubbly festivals, culinary celebrations, and social grandstands, where travelers can enjoy themed menus and diversion. These themed feasting encounters will make a bubbly and celebratory climate installed, offering travelers an interesting and charming culinary excursion.

The advancement of installed amusement and feasting assembly will proceed, with trains incorporating sight and sound encounters into the eating vehicle vibe. Brilliant feasting tables outfitted with intelligent presentations might offer amusement choices, data about menu things, and virtual culinary encounters. This intermingling of eating and diversion will change the feasting vehicle into a flexible space, taking special care of the different inclinations and interests of travelers.

Continuous input frameworks will turn out to be more modern, permitting travelers to give moment criticism on their feasting experience. Advanced criticism stages might incorporate highlights like evaluations, remarks, and studies, empowering travelers to share their contemplations and ideas. This iterative input circle will engage railroad providing food administrations to ceaselessly refine their contributions, address client inclinations, and guarantee an elevated degree of fulfillment among travelers.

Biometric confirmation advancements might be investigated to improve the security and effectiveness of locally available cooking administrations. Biometric frameworks can give secure admittance to feasting regions, smooth out registration cycles, and give customized dinner proposals in view of individual biometric information. The reconciliation of biometrics adds to a consistent and secure eating experience, lining up with the more extensive pattern of integrating trend setting innovations for traveler comfort.

Chapter 9

Conclusion

All in all, the culinary excursion through Indian rail line cooking is a rich embroidery woven with different flavors, social impacts, and developing developments. As we cross the immense railroad organization of India, the meaning of rail line providing food becomes clear not similarly for of food during movement however as a window into the country's culinary legacy, provincial variety, and the powerful combination of custom and innovation.

The verifiable development of rail route cooking in India mirrors the changing scene of the country. From the unassuming starting points of essential rewards to the present-day assorted menu contributions, the excursion reflects the development, modernization, and social reconciliation of the country. The trailblazers who established the groundwork for rail line cooking unwittingly set up for a culinary odyssey that would turn into an essential piece of the Indian rail travel insight.

The Flavor Highway, a figurative and exacting excursion, features the huge impact of flavors on Indian food and, likewise, railroad cooking. The sweet-smelling orchestra of flavors rises above provincial limits, making a binding together string that integrates the culinary encounters of travelers across different geologies. It represents the capacity of food to connect holes, interface societies, and make a common tangible encounter.

Investigation of different provincial cooking styles served on Indian trains divulges the tremendous culinary scene that traverses the subcontinent. Every locale brings its novel flavors, fixings, and cooking methods to the feasting vehicles, offering travelers a gastronomic visit that goes past the tracks. From the vigorous curries of the North to the unobtrusive coconut-injected dishes of the South, the rail route cooking menu fills in as a microcosm of India's culinary variety.

The impact of neighborhood flavors and flavors on rail route catering isn't just a gustatory encounter however a demonstration of the flexibility of Indian food. Nearby fixings and customary cooking strategies imbue credibility into the installed feasts, giving travelers a sample of the district they are crossing. It is a festival of the culinary legacy imbued in the dirt of every objective, carrying a feeling of spot to each feasting vehicle.

Accounts of famous dishes from various locales are stories of gastronomic joys as well as accounts that interface individuals with recollections, customs, and the common experience of partaking in a feast on a moving train. These dishes become social representatives, addressing the culinary personality of the districts they hail from and leaving an enduring engraving on the palates and recollections of travelers.

The Culinary Designers, the cooks and kitchen staff in the background, are the unrecognized yet truly great individuals of railroad providing food. Their aptitude, inventiveness, and commitment are the main thrusts that change the imperatives of locally available kitchens into open doors for culinary greatness. The difficulties they face, from restricted space to the requirement for large scale manufacturing, are met with creativity, guaranteeing that travelers experience the best expectations of food quality.

An in the background take a gander at the cooks and kitchen staff liable for rail line providing food uncovers a universe of accuracy, coordination, and fastidious preparation. The coordinated dance in the restricted spaces of train kitchens highlights the obligation to conveying feasts as well as critical culinary encounters. It is a demonstration of the versatility and energy that characterize the culinary experts guaranteeing the progress of railroad cooking.

Preparing and challenges looked in giving quality dinners at scale shed light on the powerful idea of railroad catering. The thorough preparation programs furnish the culinary groups with the abilities expected to explore the remarkable requests of locally available feasting. Challenges, whether calculated or culinary, are met with versatility, transforming them into open doors for consistent improvement and development.

Development in menu arranging and food readiness is at the very front of the culinary advancement on Indian trains. The coordination of innovation, high level kitchen hardware, and contemporary cooking strategies guarantees that the menu contributions stay dynamic, interesting to the developing preferences of travelers. It is an agreeable mix of custom and development, saving the credibility of provincial foods while embracing current culinary patterns.

Menu works of art, the ageless and well known dishes on rail line menus, mirror the getting through allure of specific flavors and arrangements. These dishes, established in custom, summon a feeling of sentimentality and solace for travelers. The works of art act as a culinary anchor, giving a recognizable and dearest part of the feasting experience in the midst of the steadily changing scene of menu developments.

The development of menu decisions over the course of the years reflects changing culinary patterns as well as a nuanced comprehension of traveler inclinations. The responsiveness of rail line catering administrations to the different preferences of travelers guarantees that the menu stays a unique impression of contemporary culinary sensibilities. It is a nonstop exchange among cooks and travelers, with each excursion impacting the culinary contributions on future trains.

Traveler top picks and their social importance highlight the profound association that people structure with the food they experience on trains. Certain dishes become something other than feasts; they become markers of excursions, discussions, and shared minutes. The social meaning of these top picks goes past the flavors, exemplifying the aggregate memory of train travel in India.

The operations of flavor, the many-sided snare of production network the executives and transportation, are the concealed strings that wind around together the culinary embroidery of rail route providing food. From obtaining neighborhood fixings to guaranteeing newness and quality, the coordinated factors are the foundation of a consistent and productive catering activity. It is a demonstration of the careful arranging expected to carry the substance of every district to the feasting tables on moving trains.

Strategic difficulties in shipping and serving food on moving trains uncover the intricacy of giving locally available dinners. The requirement for accuracy timing, coordination, and versatility to unanticipated conditions is a steady in the realm of railroad catering. The strategies of serving great many feasts day to day, each with its interesting prerequisites, represent the obligation to conveying an elevated requirement of administration.

Protection techniques to keep up with taste and quality stress the obligation to conveying a reliably superb eating experience. From cutting edge refrigeration frameworks to eco-accommodating bundling arrangements, the conservation strategies utilized in rail route providing food focus on life span as well as the maintenance of flavors and newness. It is a sensitive harmony among custom and innovation, guaranteeing that each chomp is an enjoyment for travelers.

Innovation and framework enhancements in food transportation signal a jump into the future for Indian railroad cooking. The coordination of trend setting innovations, from IoT-associated gadgets to shrewd kitchen hardware, upgrades effectiveness and guarantees the best expectations of food handling. The interest in foundation mirrors a guarantee to remaining at the very front of culinary development and meeting the advancing assumptions for travelers.

Stories from the storeroom vehicle, a versatile kitchen on trains, give a brief look into the core of installed culinary tasks. The storeroom vehicle is a center of action, where culinary specialists work resolutely to get ready and collect feasts that will traverse the length and expansiveness of the country. These stories are accounts of culinary ability as well as accounts of flexibility, versatility, and the quest for greatness despite challenges.

Accounts of the storage space vehicle, a versatile kitchen on trains, offer a more profound comprehension of the encounters of the staff working in this unique climate. From exploring the complexities of a moving train to dealing with the strategies of feast readiness, the storage space vehicle staff and gourmet specialists epitomize devotion and skill. Their accounts rejuvenate the human component in the background, displaying the energy that goes into each feast served ready.

Encounters of storage room vehicle staff and gourmet experts feature the special difficulties and compensations of working in a versatile kitchen. The kinship, flexibility, and relentless obligation to conveying quality dinners make a firm group that guarantees the outcome of rail route cooking. These encounters are a demonstration of the strength and collaboration that characterize the storage space vehicle staff's job in the culinary excursion on Indian trains.

Essential minutes and difficulties looked on the tracks give bits of knowledge into the flighty yet thrilling universe of rail line catering. From exploring different territories to guaranteeing the ideal conveyance of dinners, each excursion is a remarkable experience. The difficulties experienced are met with cleverness, transforming expected deterrents into potential open doors for advancement and development.

The feasting vehicle experience, a famous feature of train travel, is a demonstration of the change of installed eating into a complex and charming undertaking. The development of eating vehicle administrations on Indian trains mirrors the changing assumptions for travelers, who presently look for food as well as a vivid and pleasurable feasting experience. The eating vehicle is a social space, a culinary safe house, and an image of the developing idea of train travel in India.

Development of eating vehicle administrations on Indian trains represents the progress from essential rewards to a thorough and organized feasting experience. The feasting vehicle is presently not simply a spot to consume dinners yet an objective inside the excursion, where travelers can relish enhances, mingle, and make enduring recollections. It is an impression of the obligation to lifting the general travel insight through culinary greatness.

Extravagant and themed eating encounters presented on Indian trains reclassify the idea of installed feasting, offering travelers a sample of richness and restrictiveness. From extravagance trains with Michelin-featured cooks to themed feasting occasions that transport travelers to various culinary universes, these encounters take care of the insightful preferences of present day voyagers. It is a marriage of extravagance, development, and the immortal charm of train travel.

Traveler tributes and noteworthy feasting vehicle minutes give a brief look into the effect of culinary encounters on the general impression of train travel. The eating vehicle turns into a space where outsiders become colleagues, and dinners become shared snapshots of happiness. The tributes catch the profound reverberation of the eating vehicle, where the kinds of the excursion wait long after the train has arrived at its objective.

Taking care of different palates is a foundation of the developing culinary scene on Indian trains. The accentuation on obliging dietary inclinations and limitations guarantees that each traveler can participate in the gastronomic excursion. The inclusivity in menu contributions mirrors a consciousness of the different culinary requirements of travelers and a guarantee to giving a fantastic and customized eating experience.

Obliging dietary inclinations and limitations isn't just a culinary thought however a pledge to inclusivity. Whether travelers follow explicit weight control plans because of wellbeing reasons, strict convictions, or individual decisions, the work to give different and appropriate menu choices mirrors a client driven approach. It is an acknowledgment that the culinary excursion on Indian trains ought to take care of the differed preferences and prerequisites of a different traveler segment.

Extraordinary dinner choices and their fame epitomize the responsiveness of rail line catering administrations to the changing dietary inclinations of travelers. From veggie lover and vegetarian decisions to Jain and sans gluten choices, the menu takes special care of a range of dietary requirements. The ubiquity of these exceptional dinner choices highlights the significance of offering assorted decisions that line up with individual inclinations and limitations.

Endeavors to take care of worldwide preferences on specific courses mirror the worldwide idea of train travel in India. As trains interface various districts and states, cooking administrations perceive the different culinary assumptions for travelers. The consideration of global flavors on specific courses adds an additional layer of assortment to the installed menu, giving travelers a culinary excursion that rises above borders.

Future tracks hold the commitment of extraordinary changes in the domain of railroad catering. From digitalization and supportability drives to extravagance encounters and vivid culinary excursions, what's in store is dynamic and lively. The expectations and potential outcomes imply a culinary renaissance on Indian trains, where custom and development mix to make a consistent and magnificent gastronomic journey.

Developments in rail line catering innovation and administrations address a forward-looking methodology that embraces the capability of digitalization. From savvy menus and computer based intelligence driven personalization to contactless installments and manageability drives, these developments rethink the locally available eating experience. The incorporation of state of the art innovations prepares for a future where travelers can expect a more consistent, customized, and mechanically coordinated culinary excursion.

Supportability drives in food bundling and obtaining mark a cognizant shift towards eco-accommodating practices inside the rail route catering industry. The decrease of single-use plastics, the reception of biodegradable materials, and moral obtaining rehearses add to a more economical and mindful methodology. These drives signal a promise to ecological stewardship and line up with worldwide endeavors to make a more manageable and versatile food framework.

Expectations and opportunities for the eventual fate of Indian rail route providing food offer a brief look into a culinary scene that is dynamic, imaginative, and sensitive to the developing inclinations of travelers. The digitalization of administrations, the accentuation on manageability, the festival of neighborhood and global flavors, and the incorporation of state of the art innovations on the whole illustrate a future where the culinary excursion isn't simply a need yet a feature of train travel.

In the embroidery of Indian rail route catering, every component - from the Zest Course to the operations of flavor, from the Culinary Specialists to themed eating encounters - adds to the rich and developing story of culinary greatness. As the excursion proceeds, rail route cooking will without a doubt assume a focal part in molding the gastronomic encounters of travelers, producing recollections, and turning into a vital piece of the social texture of train travel in India.

9.1 Summarize key takeaways from the culinary journey

The culinary excursion through Indian rail route providing food unfurls as a lively embroidery woven with different flavors, social subtleties, and mechanical developments. From its verifiable advancement to the unique present and the promising future, key important points arise, epitomizing the pith of this gastronomic experience.

Authentic Development and Social Importance:

The excursion starts with a review look at the verifiable development of rail line providing food in India. From unassuming rewards to a far reaching menu addressing the social variety of the country, the culinary scene has developed couple with the development and modernization of the country. Rail line providing food serves as a functional need during movement as well as a social diplomat, acquainting travelers with the local flavors and culinary customs that characterize each stop along the tracks.

The Zest Course and Nearby Flavors:

The allegorical Zest Course becomes the dominant focal point, showing the inescapable impact of flavors on Indian cooking and, thus, railroad providing food. It rises above territorial limits, joining travelers in a common tangible encounter that commends the sweet-smelling ensemble of flavors. The accentuation on neighborhood flavors and flavors in rail line providing food goes past simple food, offering travelers a culinary identification to the different scenes and culinary legacy of the districts navigated.

Provincial Cooking styles and Notorious Dishes:

Investigation of different territorial foods served on Indian trains uncovers the culinary kaleidoscope that traverses the subcontinent. Every district contributes its special range of flavors, fixings, and culinary procedures, making a locally available menu that reflects the geological variety of India. Famous dishes arise as social milestones, becoming dinners as well as images of territorial personality and culinary pride.

Culinary Architects and In the background Authority:

The cooks and kitchen staff, frequently unrecognized yet truly great individuals, arise as Culinary Architects exploring the difficulties of bound spaces and large scale manufacturing in moving kitchens.

Their skill, devotion, and in the background dominance guarantee that travelers experience feasts as well as an ensemble of flavors coordinated with accuracy. The difficulties they face are met with development and strength, exhibiting the imaginativeness that changes installed kitchens into centers of culinary greatness.

Development in Menu Arranging and Conservation Techniques:

The advancement of railroad catering embraces development in menu arranging and food arrangement. High level kitchen gear, innovation reconciliation, and a guarantee to quality at scale rethink the culinary scene. Protection techniques, from cutting edge refrigeration to eco-accommodating bundling, guarantee that the kinds of local cooking styles are kept up with as well as celebrated. The marriage of custom and development becomes obvious, making a unique menu that requests to both the perfectionists and the daring palates.

Menu Works of art and Development Throughout the long term:

Menu works of art, ageless and darling dishes, act as anchors in the midst of the ocean of developing culinary patterns. These dishes, established in custom, bring out sentimentality and solace, giving travelers a natural and valued part of the feasting experience. The development of menu decisions over the course of the years mirrors the responsiveness of rail route taking special care of the changing preferences and inclinations of travelers, guaranteeing a dynamic and contemporary culinary excursion.

Traveler Top choices and Social Importance:

Traveler top choices arise as something beyond feasts; they become social standards implanted in the aggregate memory of train travel. These dishes, through their notoriety, rise above culinary inclinations, turning out to be important for the social texture of the rail line venture. The social meaning of traveler top choices highlights the close to home association people structure with the food they experience on trains, transforming every dinner into a common snapshot of happiness and kinship.

Planned operations of Flavor and Difficulties in Transportation:

The planned operations of flavor, a mind boggling dance of store network the board and transportation, are the inconspicuous strings that weave the culinary embroidery of rail line cooking. Exploring different landscapes, conquering strategic difficulties, and guaranteeing the convenient conveyance of feasts epitomize the intricacy of giving installed culinary encounters. The coordinated factors are a demonstration of the fastidious arranging expected to carry the pith of every district to the eating tables on moving trains.

Storeroom Vehicle Stories and Encounters of Staff:

The storeroom vehicle, a versatile kitchen on trains, arises as a focal center where culinary enchantment unfurls. Stories from the storeroom vehicle give a brief look into the unique encounters of the staff working in this difficult climate.

From exploring the complexities of a moving train to dealing with the planned operations of feast readiness, the storage space vehicle staff and gourmet specialists epitomize devotion, versatility, and skill, exhibiting the human component in the background.

Eating Vehicle Advancement and Rich Encounters:

The development of feasting vehicle administrations mirrors the changing assumptions for travelers who look for food as well as a vivid and pleasurable eating experience. The eating vehicle changes into a social space, a culinary safe house, and an image of the developing idea of train travel in India. Extravagant and themed feasting encounters reclassify the idea of installed eating, offering travelers a sample of lavishness, eliteness, and imaginative culinary excursions.

Taking care of Assorted Palates and Dietary Inclinations:

Taking care of different palates turns into a foundation of the culinary scene on Indian trains. The obligation to obliging dietary inclinations and limitations guarantees that each traveler can participate in the gastronomic excursion. The inclusivity in menu contributions mirrors a consciousness of the different culinary necessities of travelers and a pledge to giving a fantastic and customized feasting experience.

Endeavors Towards Maintainability and Future Tracks:

The fate of Indian rail route catering is set apart by a guarantee to supportability and embracing innovative progressions. Expectations and opportunities for the future grandstand a culinary renaissance where custom and development blend. Developments in rail line providing food innovation, supportability drives, and the mix of digitalization make a future where travelers can expect a consistent, customized, and mechanically coordinated culinary excursion.

9.2 Reflection on the cultural and historical significance of railway catering in India

The social and verifiable meaning of rail route catering in India is an enthralling story that unfurls as a combination of flavors, customs, and cultural changes. An excursion rises above simple food during movement; rather, it fills in as a gastronomic narrative mirroring the development of the country, the reconciliation of different societies, and the essential job that food plays in molding aggregate recollections.

At its center, the verifiable development of rail route cooking matches the development and modernization of India. From the acquaintance of fundamental rewards with the far reaching menus that address the culinary variety of the nation today, rail route cooking mirrors the evolving financial scene.

It is an impression of a country moving, interfacing individuals and societies through a common culinary encounter that crosses the length and broadness of the subcontinent.

As one dives into the rich embroidery of Indian railroad providing food, the Zest Course arises as a figurative and exacting excursion that exemplifies the quintessence of Indian cooking. The fragrant ensemble of flavors, a sign of Indian culinary legacy, turns into a bringing together string that ties travelers from various districts. The Zest Course not just acquaints voyagers with the differed kinds of the land yet additionally represents the verifiable shipping lanes that have molded the social and gastronomic scene of the country.

The investigation of assorted provincial foods served on Indian trains reveals the culinary kaleidoscope that characterizes the subcontinent. Every locale contributes its novel culinary character, offering travelers a sensorial excursion through the particular flavors, fixings, and cooking procedures of the area navigated. Rail route cooking turns into a microcosm of India's culinary variety, encouraging an appreciation for the nuanced embroidery of territorial foods.

The impact of neighborhood flavors and flavors on rail route cooking goes past a gustatory encounter; it turns into a festival of the flexibility of Indian food. Installed feasts are not simply food but rather a portrayal of the locale being crossed. Nearby fixings and conventional cooking strategies inject credibility into the culinary contributions, making a unique gastronomic encounter that resounds with travelers and interfaces them to the social underlying foundations of every objective.

Accounts of notorious dishes from various districts arise as social diplomats, conveying the legacy and customs of explicit areas. These dishes become more than culinary manifestations; they exemplify the soul of the district, filling in as markers of character and pride. Notable dishes are a demonstration of the social meaning of food, rising above its utilitarian reason to become images of territorial lavishness and variety.

The meaning of rail line catering in India reaches out past the flavors on the plate to the Culinary Architects - the gourmet experts and kitchen staff who organize the gastronomic orchestra in the background. Their job becomes urgent in conveying luscious feasts at scale as well as in saving and exhibiting the legitimacy of provincial cooking styles. The difficulties they explore, from the imperatives of locally available kitchens to the interest for large scale manufacturing, mirror their obligation to culinary greatness and add to the authentic account of railroad catering.

An in the background take a gander at the gourmet specialists and kitchen staff liable for rail route cooking discloses a universe of accuracy, coordination, and imagination. The bound spaces of train kitchens become materials where culinary skill changes difficulties into valuable open doors.

It is a demonstration of the versatility and enthusiasm of the culinary experts who work indefatigably to guarantee that each traveler encounters the best expectations of food quality.

The preparation and difficulties looked in giving quality dinners at scale become basic sections in the social account of rail line providing food. Thorough preparation programs furnish culinary groups with the abilities expected to explore the exceptional requests of installed eating. Challenges, whether calculated or culinary, are met with flexibility and development, forming the ethos of railroad providing food as a dynamic and versatile culinary excursion.

Development in menu arranging and food planning turns into an extension among custom and innovation. High level kitchen hardware, innovation combination, and inventive menu arranging guarantee that the culinary contributions advance with the changing preferences of travelers. This development turns into an impression of a general public in motion, embracing contemporary culinary patterns while protecting the credibility of conventional cooking styles.

Menu works of art, the ageless and well known dishes on rail line menus, become social anchors in the midst of the always changing scene of culinary patterns. These works of art, established in custom, bring out wistfulness and solace for travelers. The development of menu decisions throughout the years turns into a demonstration of the responsiveness of railroad providing food administrations to the powerful inclinations of travelers, delineating a culinary exchange that traverses ages.

The social meaning of traveler top choices and their effect on the general travel experience highlights the profound association people structure with the food they experience on trains. Certain dishes become inseparable from the actual excursion, adding to an aggregate memory of train travel in India. The social reverberation of traveler top picks reaches out past the culinary domain, exemplifying the quintessence of shared encounters and public happiness.

The planned operations of flavor, the multifaceted snare of production network the board, and the difficulties in shipping and serving food on moving trains uncover the intricacy innate in giving locally available feasts. The fastidious arranging expected to carry the substance of every locale to the feasting tables on moving trains turns into a demonstration of the obligation to conveying an elevated expectation of administration. The strategies of flavor not just grandstand the functional ability of rail line catering yet in addition feature job as a social channel brings the different culinary legacy of India to travelers.

The protection strategies utilized to keep up with taste and quality mirror a sensitive harmony among custom and innovation. From cutting edge refrigeration frameworks to eco-accommodating bundling arrangements, these techniques guarantee that the kinds of territorial cooking styles are held as well as celebrated.

Conservation turns into a social obligation to protecting the credibility of each dish, permitting travelers to encounter the genuine substance of the locales they cross.

Innovation and framework enhancements in food transportation address a jump into the future for Indian railroad catering. The combination of cutting edge innovations, from IoT-associated gadgets to savvy kitchen hardware, improves proficiency and guarantees the best expectations of sanitation. This interest in framework mirrors a promise to remaining at the very front of culinary development and meeting the developing assumptions for travelers.

9.3 Closing thoughts on the fusion of travel and gastronomy in Indian railways.

The combination of movement and gastronomy inside the domain of Indian rail routes embodies a story that rises above simple transportation; it is an odyssey of flavors, a festival of variety, and a social undertaking on tracks. As we examine the interaction of culinary greatness and the excursion through different scenes, shutting considerations arise on the significant effect this combination has on the shared awareness of travelers and the more extensive social scene.

At its heart, the culinary excursion through Indian rail lines is a tribute to the rich woven artwork of the country's culinary legacy. The blend of territorial cooking styles, notable dishes, and the fragrant ensemble of flavors changes each train compartment into a versatile gastronomic safe house. The rail routes become a conductor, interfacing travelers not exclusively to their objections yet to the horde enhances that characterize the subcontinent. This mixture is in excess of a culinary encounter; it is an excursion into the substance of India's different culinary scene.

The Zest Course, both allegorical and strict, epitomizes the combination of movement and gastronomy. It represents the noteworthy shipping lanes that formed India's culinary personality while filling in as a binding together string associating travelers from various districts. The smells and kinds of flavors become the language expressed across the different territories navigated by the rail routes. The Zest Course, inside the setting of rail line cooking, changes each excursion into a tangible investigation, making a permanent connection between the demonstration of voyaging and the flavors experienced en route.

Territorial cooking styles arise as social representatives, welcoming travelers to participate in a gastronomic excursion through the different scenes of India. The cautiously organized menus reflect the culinary wealth of every locale as well as the social subtleties implanted in the selection of fixings, cooking methods, and show.

Through these menus, the railroads become a vessel for social trade, encouraging an appreciation for the culinary variety that characterizes India's multi-layered personality.

Famous dishes from various districts become more than dinners; they are images of local pride and personality. Whether it's the sweet-smelling biryanis of Hyderabad, the fiery curries of South India, or the delicious kebabs of the North, each dish recounts a story. The combination of these notable dishes with the actual excursion raises the demonstration of eating on a train to a social encounter. Travelers become members in a gastronomic story that unfurls with each passing mile, making recollections that wait long after the excursion finishes up.

The Culinary Architects, the cooks and kitchen staff in the background, arise as overlooked yet truly great individuals in this combination of movement and gastronomy. Their mastery, flexibility, and obligation to conveying excellent dinners at scale guarantee that the gastronomic excursion isn't simply delightful yet additionally consistent. The difficulties they face in the restricted spaces of moving kitchens become open doors for development, exhibiting the dominance expected to organize an ensemble of flavors in a hurry.

Development in menu arranging and food planning turns into a main thrust in the combination of movement and gastronomy. The joining of cutting edge kitchen gear, innovation driven personalization, and economical practices reclassify the culinary scene on Indian trains. The marriage of custom and development guarantees that travelers experience the immortal works of art as well as contemporary culinary patterns, denoting the rail lines as a powerful center point of gastronomic investigation.

The development of menu decisions throughout the long term highlights the responsiveness of rail line taking special care of the powerful inclinations of travelers. It mirrors a constant exchange between culinary practice and developing preferences. The menu turns into a living report, adjusting to changing culinary patterns while protecting the credibility of immortal top picks. This development upgrades the combination of movement and gastronomy, making each excursion a novel investigation of flavors that reflects the moving sense of taste of a different country.

Traveler top picks, well established in social importance, enhance the combination of movement and gastronomy. These dishes rise above their culinary allure, becoming social standards that interface travelers to the embodiment of a locale. The demonstration of enjoying these top picks turns into a common encounter, cultivating a feeling of local area among explorers. The social reverberation of traveler top choices changes the demonstration of feasting into a mutual festival, building up the indivisible connection among movement and gastronomy.

The coordinated operations of flavor, the complicated arranging expected to ship and serve food on moving trains, add one more layer to the combination of movement and gastronomy. It represents the obligation to conveying a credible culinary encounter no matter what the difficulties presented by the powerful idea of train travel. The operations become a demonstration of the commitment of railroad providing food administrations to guaranteeing that every traveler partakes in a gastronomic excursion that is however smooth as it seems to be tasty.

The storage space vehicle, a portable kitchen on trains, arises as a vital participant in the combination of movement and gastronomy. It is a unique space where culinary enchantment unfurls, and the difficulties of a moving climate are met with creativity. The encounters of storeroom vehicle staff and cooks give an in the background look into the energy and mastery that go into creating every dinner. The storeroom vehicle turns into an image of flexibility, guaranteeing that the combination of movement and gastronomy stays a work of art instead of a calculated test.

The eating vehicle experience, developing from essential rewards to an organized feasting issue, means the zenith of the combination of movement and gastronomy. It changes the demonstration of eating into a social and tangible occasion, welcoming travelers to wait and relish the kinds of the excursion. Sumptuous and themed eating encounters presented on Indian trains reclassify the idea of installed feasting, hoisting it to a domain of lavishness and restrictiveness. The feasting vehicle turns into an image of the developing idea of train travel, where gastronomy isn't just a need however a basic piece of the general insight.

Taking special care of different palates and obliging dietary inclinations exemplify inclusivity inside the combination of movement and gastronomy. The accentuation on giving a delightful and customized eating experience guarantees that each traveler, paying little heed to dietary limitations or inclinations, can participate in the gastronomic excursion. The inclusivity in menu contributions turns into a festival of variety, transforming every dinner into a snapshot of divided happiness between travelers with shifting preferences.

Endeavors to take special care of worldwide preferences on specific courses mirror the worldwide idea of train travel in India. The consideration of worldwide flavors adds an additional layer of assortment to the gastronomic excursion, making an encounter that rises above public lines. It builds up the possibility that the combination of movement and gastronomy is an all inclusive language that interfaces people from various regions of the planet.

As we peer into what's in store tracks, the combination of movement and gastronomy takes on new aspects. Digitalization, supportability drives, and extravagance encounters become essential parts of this combination.

The combination of state of the art innovations guarantees a more consistent, customized, and mechanically incorporated culinary excursion. Maintainability drives signal a pledge to capable works on, lining up with worldwide endeavors to make a more manageable and versatile food framework. Extravagance encounters and vivid culinary excursions propose a future where the combination of movement and gastronomy turns out to be much more experiential and custom-made to the insightful preferences of present day voyagers.

www.ingramcontent.com/pod-product-compliance
Lightning Source LLC
LaVergne TN
LVHW010649200726
843507LV00011B/1784